# Madeira

**120th anniversary**

**Berlitz**

- A ☞ in the text denotes a highly recommended sight
- A complete A–Z of practical information starts on p.103
- Extensive mapping on cover flaps

## Berlitz Publishing Company, Inc.

Princeton   Mexico City   Dublin   Eschborn   Singapore

| | |
|---|---|
| Text: | Paul Murphy |
| Editors: | Donald Greig, Claire Evans Calder |
| Photography: | Paul Murphy |
| Layout: | Media Content Marketing, Inc. |
| Cartography: | Falk-Verlag Munich |

Thanks to the Portuguese National Tourist Office, the Funchal
Tourist Office and the Porto Santo Tourist Office, especially Pilar
Pereira, Vanda Gonçalves and Rita Ornelas respectively, and the
Blandy Travel Agency for their invaluable help in the preparation of
this guide.

*Found an error we should know about? Our editor would be happy
to hear from you, and a postcard would do. Although we make every
effort to ensure the accuracy of all the information in this book,
changes do occur.*

ISBN 2-8315-6472-7
Revised 1998 – First Printing May 1998

Printed in Switzerland by Weber SA, Bienne
019/805 REV

# CONTENTS

# MADEIRA

# MADEIRA AND THE MADEIRANS

**M**adeira is an island garden floating in the Atlantic, some 445 km (275 miles) to the north of Tenerife and 965 km (600 miles) southwest of Lisbon. It is only 500 km (310 miles) off the coast of Africa, and every so often a hot wind called the *leste* blows in, just as a reminder. This is an exception to the weather, however, and to the island's spirit in general, for Madeira is a place of moderation in most things, a haven of civilized peace, where respect and Old-World manners have yet to become outdated.

Formed from volcanic eruptions many millions of years ago, Madeira, like the Canary Islands, is an archipelago. In structure, the land is akin to an iceberg, with massive mountains reaching high up through the clouds and forming merely the tip of a much greater submerged mass. Only one other island in the group is inhabited—the barely discovered holiday hideaway of Porto Santo. Christopher Columbus visited Porto Santo in the second half of the 15th century, when he married the governor's daughter.

Just as then, the islands of Madeira and Porto Santo are still parts of Portugal. Madeira is very small—only 56 km (35 miles) long and 21 km (13 miles) wide—but don't even think about driving around it in a day. Contorted during the volcanic holocaust which created the island in the first place, the terrain is so mountainous, and its roads so tortuous, that distances are magnified in terms of both time and effort.

This can breed a certain insularity, and some of the villagers have never been as far as Funchal, while the thought of stepping off Madeira altogether is totally incomprehensible. Yet young and upwardly mobile islanders do go off in search of fortune, and the most successful return from Brazil, Venezuela, or South Africa to build the sumptuous villas that overlook the Bay of Funchal.

Given Madeira's history of emigration and return, of welcoming visiting merchants and seafarers and, during a brief period of occupation, a garrison of British troops, it comes as

---

## Desertas and Selvagens

In addition to Madeira and Porto Santo, the Madeiran archipelago comprises another five islands and numerous minor rocks and reefs, all of which once constituted part of a land mass that also included the Canary Islands and the Azores. The islands fall into two groups: the Ilhas Desertas (desert isles) and Ilhas Selvagens (wild or savage islands). The former consist of three islands, the nearest being 12 km (19 miles) southeast of Madeira. However, these desert islands are far from the Robinson Crusoe idyll; they are barren and inhospitable to the point where, aside from the occasional goat and rabbit, the most notable land creature is a large, poisonous black spider.

The sea life around the islands is a different story, however. Dolphins and turtles are occasionally spotted, and there is a colony of monk seals. Birdwatchers will relish the opportunity to see shearwaters and petrels. Marine biologists and nature conservationists are the only regular human visitors, for even though excursion boats frequently make trips to these isles in summer, landing is restricted to authorized persons only.

Meanwhile, the two Selvagens Islands, usually known as Grande (large) and Pequena (small), are Madeiran only in name (they are actually closer to Tenerife), and lie 285 km (177 miles) to the south. Like the Desertas, they are uninhabited and devoted to nature conservation.

no surprise that the Madeirans are a cosmopolitan mix. Here on this island are gathered faces of the world, from the distinctive, dark North African complexions to the blonde, blue-eyed northern Europeans.

Nearly a third of the population congregates in Funchal, the island's capital and only city of any note, which is built on picturesque hills sloping down to a steep bay. You may find that you prefer this busy place from afar, rather than close up. It certainly has character and charm, but it is also cursed—like most cities elsewhere in the world—by noise and traffic. This is where cruise-ship passengers step ashore for a brief flurry of sightseeing and shopping. Less fleeting visitors are pampered in the large and famous hotels along the city's western seafront. Tourism has been so successful here in recent years that the new Tourist Zone has sprung up, which to the traditional visitor to Madeira, used to old-world hotels and distinguished *quintas* (19th-century estate villas), must look rather vulgar and out of place.

It would be a shame to take Funchal for Madeira, however. For many visitors, the island starts for real outside the town, where the magnificent flora for which Madeira is renowned amply justifies its nickname of "God's botanic garden." Here, you will find all the best gardens within a short bus or taxi ride of the capital.

*The stunning northwest coast between Porto Moniz and Seixal.*

Agriculture is still the dominating influence on the landscape. Depending on the altitude and whether you happen to be on the warm south coast or the marginally cooler north coast, you will see either terrace upon terrace of bananas, or the grapevines which go to produce the fortified wine that has made the island famous. In the background there is often a stunning vista of mountain peaks and hillsides plummeting down to the sea, and lush green valleys dotted about with little white houses with red-tiled roofs. Strategically situated look-out points (*miradouros*) mean that you can pull over safely, even on hairpin bends, and enjoy these magical panoramas.

By far the best way to see the countryside is to walk, and, fortunately, Madeira boasts a system that makes this possible for all ages and abilities. Irrigation channels, known as *levadas*, criss-cross the island on gentle gradients and have footpaths running along their entire length.

With wonderful scenery and a climate that rarely fluctuates from a delightful, suntanning warmth, perhaps it is a little much to expect nature to bestow Madeira with miles of beach as well. Instead, Porto Santo has a beach, running the length of its south coast, although this smaller island cannot claim the variety of natural attractions of Madeira. There is an excellent lido on the main is-

*Across the roofs of old-world Madeira.*

*Children at the flower festival.*

land, however, as well as a handful of pebbly beaches for both the young and young-at-heart. Perhaps it's not such a bad thing—as some people say—that Madeira's shoreline crashes so violently into the ocean, for a Madeira with long, sandy beaches would surely not have been capable of staving off the attentions of the mass-tourist market as successfully as it has been able to do so far.

The times are beginning to change, though, as Funchal's new Tourist Zone testifies. The typical visitor is still older and wealthier than you will find in most holiday destinations, but nowadays there is a fair sprinkling of younger people, too. New lido facilities have been completed, and the island's nightlife (if not yet in the Ibiza mould) is improving.

But what of the Madeirans themselves? Being of Portuguese descent, it is no surprise that they are, generally speaking, a quiet and reserved people. Add to this geographical isolation and the difficulties of a harsh, agricultural existence (there is precious little machinery to help in the tiny terraced fields), and you could forgive the islanders if they seemed less than welcoming.

Instead you will find a genuinely cheerful and friendly people who will often go to great lengths to help visitors, and all for the sake of good old-fashioned hospitality, not just a tip. In spite of a 12-month season and many years of tourism, Madeirans are refreshingly free of the kind of unpleasantness which can be so common in other popular holiday destinations.

For many, a week here is ideal; after that, some say, you start to run out of ideas (by which they usually mean man-made attractions). The whole allure of Madeira, however, is not to look for such attractions in the first place. The beauty of the island and the charm of the easy-going people are appealing enough in themselves to satisfy the major hard core of Madeira's loyal visitors. The island *isn't* everyone's cup of tea, which is exactly why it is loved by so many others.

*Madiera is somewhere to relax—take a break in Funchal's Jardim São Francisco.*

# A BRIEF HISTORY

**A**s befits an island stranded in the middle of the ocean, Madeira's origins are shrouded in the sort of mystery that invites legends to grow and the imagination to run riot. Is the archipelago the remains of Atlantis, or part of a land mass that once joined the continents of Europe and America? And who was it exactly that first set eyes on Madeira—the Phoenicians or that intrepid voyager, St. Brendan? Madeira's history leaves itself wide open to such unabashed speculation.

## The Portuguese Step Ashore

The official recorded history of the Madeiran archipelago starts only in relatively recent times, in 1418, at the beginning of the golden age of Portuguese discoveries around the world. Under the leadership of Henry the Navigator, caravels set out from the Algarve in search of foreign lands, fame, and wealth. So it was that João Gonçalves Zarco, sailing in the service of Prince Henry, made the first of many famous Portuguese discoveries that were to culminate a century later in Magellan's historic circumnavigation of the globe.

Some stories say that Zarco knew precisely where he was heading, having learned of the existence of Madeira from a Castilian source. Besides, the waters of the Canary Islands, only 445 km (275 miles) to the south, had been busy shipping lanes for very nearly a century. Surely, they reasoned, someone must have happened upon the Madeiran archipelago during that time.

Others claim that Zarco was in fact heading for Guinea, and it was merely by chance that a storm carried him onto the beach of Porto Santo. If this was the case, then he was extremely fortunate, for he managed to land on the only large, sandy beach for hundreds of miles around. Little wonder he subsequently named it Porto Santo (Holy Port).

The following year Zarco returned to claim the island he had seen from Porto Santo, and with him went Tristão Vaz Teixeira (pronounced Tayj-air-a, with a soft j) and Bartolomeu Perestrelo. Around 1419 they became the first men to set foot on the island (officially at least) and named it *Ilha da Madeira*, "Island of Timber," after its forested appearance. The Portuguese Crown, no doubt delighted with their first important discovery, immediately embarked on a programme of colonization. Zarco and Teixeira were subsequently appointed co-governors of Madeira, while Perestrelo was awarded Porto Santo.

## Starting from Scratch

Although there is some controversy over who stepped ashore on Madeira first (see page 15), it is fact that whoever it was discovered no sign of habitation—no Stone-Age natives, as the Spanish found on the Canary Islands, and no monuments to the past, as on the Balearics.

Occupation of Madeira thus started in the early 1420s with just what the colonists could carry, although there was plenty of water, pouring down from the mountains, and more timber than anyone knew what

*Infante Dom Henrique (or Prince Henry), whose vision led to the discovery of Madeira.*

to do with. The task of clearing the land for agriculture was undertaken by setting fire to massive tracts of forest. Some stories say this got out of hand (which is believable, since this is a problem on the island even today), and tell of a great fire that burned for between five and seven years. More prosaically, this is probably the length of time it actually took the settlers to clear the land. Either way, the fire provided the soil with a rich ash fertilizer, which complemented the luxuriant growing conditions of tropical sun and plentiful water.

The Portuguese now realized that a valuable economic opportunity was to hand, and ordered Malvasia grapes from Crete in addition to sugar cane from Italy in an effort to provide the first cash crops. Two problems remained, however. The first

## First Man on Madeira?

According to an old legend, the first man on Madeira was not the Portuguese adventurer, João Gonçalves Zarco, but an Englishman named Robert Machim (or Machin).

One version of the story is that Machim was a knight at the court of Edward III and wanted to marry above his class, to a girl named Anne d'Arfet (or Anne of Hertford). The young lovers defied convention and boarded a ship for France, but this was thrown severely off course and the pair ended up shipwrecked on Madeira. She died of exposure soon afterwards and he buried her by the bay where they had landed. He too died (of a broken heart) and was buried alongside her by members of the same shipwrecked crew, who eventually escaped on a log raft and recounted the tragic tale.

Zarco apparently heard of the legend and, when he discovered the island, found the grave of the couple, so naming the place Machico in honour of Machin. The couple's last resting place is, by legend, beneath the chapel of Senhor dos Milagres on the eastern side of Machico Bay.

was finding enough level ground on which crops could be grown, and the second was how to get the necessary water to them. Sheer hard work created the flat ground, as the early settlers built the terraces on the steep slopes that we still see today. No machinery was used then, nor is it practical now; the hillsides are too steep and the pockets of land too small.

The problem of watering the crops was solved by the irrigation system known as *levadas* (famous nowadays for great walking opportunities). These simply-designed water channels were built largely by slave labourers, mostly from Africa, who also worked on the sugar plantations. Sugar was the luxury item of this period (trade with Britain and Flanders was brisk), and the new Madeirans proved very skillful in the art of wine-making, too. The island became significant to the

*Trading sugarcane and wine helped to make life sweeter for the early Madeirans.*

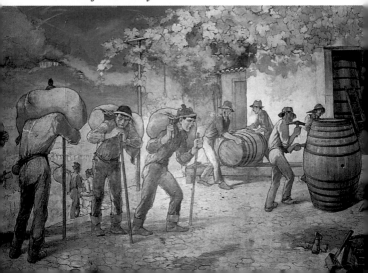

Portuguese economy and its population began to grow. By the middle of the 15th century it numbered some 800 families, and a census of 1514 records 5,000 inhabitants.

Around 1478, Madeira welcomed a visitor who, one way or another, would assist the future wine trade of the island. Columbus sailed to Madeira on an assignment to buy sugar cane. His trip was not totally successful, as money failed to arrive for part of the shipment, but he returned six years later, by which time evidence suggests that he was an experienced sugarcane merchant. It was his discovery of the New World, however, which was to bring prosperity to Madeira's wine trade, for the island's location on the great East-West route meant that ships would stop off to take on food, water, and the valuable trading commodity of Madeira wine.

Columbus had his eye on more than sugar in Madeira. He married Dona Filipa Moniz (Perestrelo), daughter of Porto Santo's first governor, and—it is claimed—lived on the island for a period, fathering a son into the bargain. Even today, there are those on Porto Santo who will tell you that it was due to his time spent here that Christopher Columbus learned navigation techniques and the ways of the ocean, and found the inspiration to undertake his voyage of 1492.

## Invaders

In 1566 Madeira suffered its worst man-made disaster. Well aware of the island's burgeoning supplies, the French pirate Bertrand de Montluc sailed into Funchal harbour with his 11-galleon armada and 1,300 men. He then unleashed a 16-day reign of terror that left 300 Madeirans dead, stocks of sugar destroyed, and the island plundered. By the time Lisbon was able to come to the rescue, the pirates had long fled (though Montluc himself had been killed during the raid). As a result of the attack, Porto Santo, which had also been scourged by these villains of the seas, went on to build castles and early warning systems, which allowed the citizens to defend themselves or flee as and when necessary. An invasion of even greater significance followed in 1580, when Philip II of Spain proclaimed himself king of Portugal and marched his armies across the border. The Spanish remained for another 60 years, during which time Madeira became a Spanish territory.

In the 16th century, Madeira lost its dominance of the sugarcane industry to another Portuguese colony, Brazil. Moreover, sugar cane had taken a hefty toll on the Madeiran soil and many exhausted plantations were supplanted by less-demanding vines. Sugarcane continues to be grown today (for molasses and the brandy-like *aguardente*), but has long ceased to be the major crop.

## The British Are Coming!

Britain's traditional links with Madeira began as early as the 17th century, when, in 1662, Charles II married Portugal's Catherine of Bragança. A provision written into the bride's dowry granted special favours to British settlers on Madeira, and it is said that had Charles been a little more hard-nosed, the Portuguese may even have agreed to hand over the island to Britain in its entirety.

Additionally, both Madeira and Britain benefited from a new regulation that governed the shipment of Madeira wine, which meant that it became the only wine which could be exported directly to the British sections of the Western hemisphere (providing, of course, it was carried by a British vessel). All other wines had to be shipped to the Americas via a British harbour. These trading rights attracted more Britons to the island, who founded dynastic families that, until comparatively recently, constituted the island's élite. Profits from

*This statue Christopher Columbus in Funchal is a reminder of this famous explorer's venture to Madeira.*

wine were huge, and by 1800 exports had reached nine million bottles per year. Many of the *quintas* (villas) which we can still see today are an elegant legacy of that time.

British troops were moved into the island in 1801 to protect against a possible invasion by the French, but were withdrawn following the Treaty of Amiens in 1802. During their stay they made many friends among the islanders. In 1807, the Treaty was put in jeopardy and the troops returned, staying until 1814. Although it is said that the relationship was not as good as formerly, many of the garrison remained and married into the community.

## War and Pestilence

The second half of the 19th century was most memorable for natural disasters. In 1852 the precious vines were blighted by mildew, wiping out an estimated 90 percent of the total crop. Even worse was to come in 1873, however, when the dreaded disease phylloxera destroyed the remainder of the vines. The potato and sugar crops were also badly affected during this period, and on top of all this, in 1856, cholera claimed the lives of up to 7,000 Madeirans.

The start of the 20th century brought World War I, and Portugal took up arms in 1916. Inevitably, Madeira's strategic position for Atlantic shipping did not escape the notice of the German High Command, and in December of that year a German submarine bombarded the harbour of Funchal and sank three French ships.

*Reid's Hotel has hosted many famous travellers, such as Winston Churchill and George Bernard Shaw.*

# Modern Times

As mainland Portugal lurched into a political and economic crisis that brought down the country's republican government, Madeira was busy looking after distinguished visitors and developing the beginnings of today's tourist trade. It had, in effect, been doing this since the middle of the 19th century, attracting wealthy British sun-lovers, minor royalty, and aristocrats from many countries. The island's celebrated Reid's Hotel had opened its doors in 1890, and a seaplane service started operating from Lisbon in 1921. Madeira was given further cachet when the last of the Austro-Hungarian emperors, Charles I of Austria (also Charles IV of Hungary), chose Madeira as his home in exile after the war.

## Reid's Hotel

If there is one building that sums up the love affair between the British and Madeira over the last 100 years, then it must be Reid's. William Reid from Scotland was responsible for building this splendid, cream-coloured structure, and when it opened in 1890, it had no competitors for the best view of the bay. Since 1937 it has been in the hands of the famous Blandys, one of Madeira's oldest and most distinguished families, who also have a stake in the Cliff Bay Hotel next door.

Reid's has always been the last word in understated luxury, and its guest list includes famous Britons (such as Winston Churchill and George Bernard Shaw) and members of foreign royalty. If you cannot afford to stay at the hotel, the next best thing is afternoon tea on the terrace above the bay (although even that will set you back the price of a meal elsewhere). You can then wander around the beautiful 4 hectare (10 acre) gardens.

Portugal now gained a new ruler and dictator in ex-Minister of Finance Dr. António Salazar. For all his introspective, harsh policies and political failings, Salazar did at least succeed in keeping Portugal out of World War II, and this fact, combined with his tight financial control, helped the country to regain economic stability. Following a bloodless coup in 1974, Salazar's successor, Dr. Caetano, was overthrown and free elections were held. Madeira was then granted autonomy, in addition to the right to set its own taxes and to send a deputation to the Portuguese government.

In 1986 Portugal, and therefore also Madeira, joined the European Community (now the European Union, or EU). Money from this source has been invested in the island's roads and fishing industry, but the long-term effect of EU membership on its agriculture may be detrimental. Tourism, however, seems set to be the island's primary industry until well into the next millennium.

## Cruise Passengers

Madeira has welcomed many distinguished sea voyagers in its long tradition of hospitality, including, in 1815, the defeated Napoleon Bonaparte. En route to exile on St. Helena in the South Atlantic, his ship anchored to take on supplies. The only visitor allowed aboard was the British consul, who graciously presented Britain's old enemy with bottles of vintage Madeira wine to help while away his confinement. (Napoleon, to his credit, responded with gold coins.) History just about repeated itself after the 1974 coup, when the deposed Portugese leaders, ex-President Tomás and Prime Minister Caetano, also stopped at Madeira en route to their exile in Brazil. This time, however, the defeated party was allowed ashore, but only to be locked up in the São Lourenço fortress.

# WHERE TO GO

## FUNCHAL

Funchal, the Madeiran capital, is the one and only town of any size on the island, or indeed in the archipelago. With a population of 120,000 it may sound surprisingly large, but in fact you can walk across the centre (from east to west) in 10 to 15 minutes. Exploring inland to the north is not as easy on foot, as you will soon find the streets become very steep. Nevertheless, walking remains the only practical way to see Funchal, for the narrow, cobbled streets were never meant for motor vehicles, and traffic here can be a nightmare.

To get your bearings, walk out on the jetty known as the **Pontinha** and see Funchal as if you were arriving at the island on a cruise ship. Built in 1962, the Pontinha tunnels its way straight through the middle of the old fortress (Nossa

*Funchal Bay is a magnificent sight from any angle.*

Senhora da Conceição), which until then was perched on top of a tiny island known as Looe Rock. From here, it's the view towards land that catches your attention: squat white houses with red terracotta roofs climb up steeply through the tropical greenery, which tumbles down towards the spacious bay.

Look up above the town to the mountains (the weather may change while you watch). The clear, blue sky of only ten minutes ago has been invaded by clumps of increasingly dark clouds, which cascade down the hillsides and now hover menacingly above the town of Monte, just north of Funchal.

Look back towards the sea and you may well see fishing boats heading round the breakwater point, pursued by flocks of screeching gulls. Alternatively, there could be a cruise-liner, or, if you are lucky, one of the tall ships that call here regularly. Somewhat more prosaically, you will notice that the port also harbours oil tankers, dredgers, and the occasional warship. With the exception of ocean liners and picturesque fishing boats, Funchal is very much a working port (handling containerized freight) and is also home to a small oil terminal. (Watch out for heavy lorries along the jetty.)

By the time you've walked back to the main promenade, just past the Marina, you will probably already have gained a fair impression of Funchal. It is a town that is simultaneously both historic and modern, geared very much to the needs of its own people as well as to those of the admiring visitors it receives every year.

## The Centre of Town

The dominant building on the seafront is the **Palácio de São Lourenço** (Fortress of St. Lawrence). Built in the 16th century, it previously guarded the bay against pirate ships—you can still see the ancient cannons poking through crenellations in the walls. White-gloved sentries with automatic machine guns guard the fort's main gate, for this is now the residence of Madeira's military governors. Although the main building is not open to the public, the official residence of the Portuguese government is open for occasional, prearranged, guided tours (see TOURIST INFORMATION OFFICES on page 127). You can also stroll up Avenida Zarco and, on the square off Avenida Arriaga, visit a couple of side rooms and learn a little about the fort's history.

At the intersection of avenidas Zarco and Arriaga stands a statue of Madeira's discoverer, João Gonçalves Zarco—who is often referred to as the "First Captain." The statue, some 60 years old, is in need of restoration to redress the poor man's severely blackened eyes. The imposing **Palácio do Governo Regional**, the administrative headquarters of Madeira, rises behind him, arranged around shady, tiled patios.

*View of the center of town and the bustling Avenida do Infante.*

Continue up Avenida Zarco until you get to Rua da Carreira, a bustling street that is typical of the island, full of interesting, old-fashioned shops and buildings. It is particularly noteworthy for the cheap restaurants that cater primarily for city workers, but also satisfy a good number of tourists. A few yards left is the **Photographia Museu Vicentes** (Vicente Pho-

**25**

tography Museum). It is easy to miss, but once you have spotted it, cross the street and look back at the faded, ancient sign and the colonnades on the wall above. The narrow entrance squeezes past a bookshop and opens out into a delightful, plant-filled patio. This was the first public photo studio to be opened in Portugal (during the 1850s), and some of the props on display are amusingly quaint. In addition to the varied selection of memorabilia and antique photographic equipment, don't miss having a flick through the albums of photographs of old Madeira, dating from 1884.

*Entrada livre –*
**admission free**
*é proibido tirar*
*fotographias –* **no**
**cameras allowed.**

Head back in the opposite direction on Rua da Carreira until you reach the **Praça do Município**, the town's handsome main square, with a mosaic black-and-white surface and major buildings on three sides. Entering the square, you will see the 17th-century **Igreja do Colégio** (Collegiate Church) to the left. A spacious and airy old place, it's decorated with 17th- and 18th-century tiles, paintings, and gilt-wood carving. The adjacent college, founded by the Jesuits, served as a barracks for British troops in the 19th century.

Straight ahead on the square stands the **Câmara Municipal** (Town Hall), which occupies a former

*The Praça do Município*
*— the cathedral spire*
*stands tall in front of the*
*the Museu de Arte Sacra.*

*Great Flemish art from the Museu de Arte Sacre: S. Pedro (St. Peter) by an unknown artist.*

18th-century palace. Don't miss the graceful, 19th-century statue of *Leda and the Swan* in the inner courtyard. The statue used to be in the old fish market—a fact corroborated by the tile panel outside the present market (see page 33). The Town Hall also houses a small museum (**Museu da Cidade do Funchal**), though its exhibits are of limited interest.

On the square's third side, and regarded as considerably more worthwhile by many, is the **Museu de Arte Sacra** (Museum of Sacred Art). This is also housed in what was an 18th-century palace, formerly the Bishop of Funchal's residence. The outstanding works of this collection are a dozen or so 15th- and 16th-century Flemish paintings, regarded as the richest in Portugal and rare even in the rest of Europe. The colours are as vibrant as if they had been painted only yesterday, and the splendid background detail on many of them is of almost as much interest as the main subject. These were bought by Funchal's wealthy sugar merchants, who during the 16th century traded their "white gold" for principal art treasures of the day. The back door of the museum leads on to Rua do Bispo (Street of the Bishop), and both this and the parallel street, Rua Queimada Cima, are worth exploring.

Rua João Tavira leads down to the end of Avenida Arriaga and Funchal's principal landmark, the **Sé** (cathedral). Although modest as cathedrals go, by Funchal's low-rise standards it is very imposing. The cathedral's interior is considerably more impressive than the plain frontage, for dating from the early 16th-century, the Sé boasts a splendid ceiling of Hispano-Arabic ivory and juniper. Note the blue-and-gold carved choir stalls.

**Avenida Arriaga** is particularly pretty during late spring, when the jacaranda trees are in full blossom. Along here you will find the helpful tourist information office and, just next door, the **São Francisco Wine Lodge**, an atmospheric place built on the site of a Franciscan monastery 150 years ago. Wine isn't actually made here any more, but you can go on a tour of the lodge and the wine cellars to learn all about the island's eponymous golden drink. A video introduction is followed by a tour of the ageing room, cooperage, museum, and the tasting room.

Next door to here is the small but lush **Jardim de São Francisco**, the perfect place to escape the noise and traffic fumes of Funchal. Exotic trees and flowers are mingled with

*The glorious carved choir stalls shine amidst the gloomy interior of Funchal's cathedral.*

statuary, and black swans glide across a small pond. Year-round concerts are put on in an auditorium at the back of the park, while on the opposite side to the wine lodge is an old Scottish kirk (church), another indicator of the strong British influence on the island's development. Opposite the park is the **Teatro Municipal** (Municipal Theatre), a miniature Victorian gem put to regular good use as a concert venue.

*The shady courtyard of the São Francisco Wine Lodge is a cool retreat on a hot summer day.*

The adjacent Bar de Teatro, a good retreat for both food and music, is favoured by students, bohemian types, and tourists. The incongruous but elegant car showroom next door was once the Chamber of Commerce and is worth noting for its fine blue-and-white *azulejo* (tile) vignettes, which depict scenes from old Madeira.

## A Walk Uphill

Just a couple of hundred yards north of the São Francisco gardens, the land begins to rise sharply. Off Rua da Carreira is Calçada Santa Clara, a picturesque hill full of interest. At the junction with Rua Mouraria is the **Museu Municipal**, yet another 18th-century aristocratic home that has been turned into a museum (entrance on Rua Mouraria). On the ground floor you will find a modest, though well-lit, aquarium showing the sealife of Madeira, while upstairs more of the same is displayed in a thoroughly old-fashioned collection of stuffed local sea and land creatures. It's a good place for younger children. Now return to the hill: on the opposite side to the museum building you will discover the charming church of **São Pedro**, which is decorated with *azulejos* and a painted ceiling, the whole in characteristic Madeiran style.

A few yards farther up the hill is the **Casa Museu Frederico de Freitas**, one of the most enjoyable and underrated attractions in Funchal. The collections include paintings of old Madeira by 19th-century English artists and the apartments of a well-to-do 18th-century Madeiran household. Unfortunately, the museum is closed indefinitely for restoration.

*The Hospício da Princesa Funchal continues to help the sick, while keeping the memory of Princess Maria Amelia.*

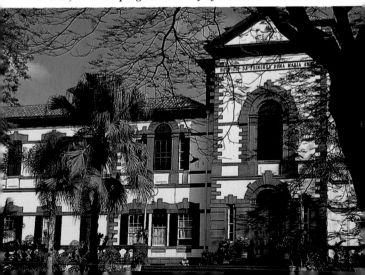

Continue uphill to the **Convento de Santa Clara**, built in the 15th century and extended two centuries later. It's now a school run by Franciscan nuns, you will probably only get to see the convent church. This is a splendid building, with walls completely covered by rare, 17th-century *azulejos* in geometric patterns, and with a fine painted ceiling. The island's discoverer, Zarco, is buried beneath the altar, but the memorial to him vanished long ago. The tomb at the back of the church belongs to members of his family (despite some guides' affirmations that this is the tomb of Zarco). If you are fortunate enough to secure a behind-the-scenes tour, you will see a copy of the tomb, which is surprisingly plain. Enquire at the tourist office, or directly, by ringing the bell at the gates, if your Portuguese is up to it.

---

## The Hospital on the Hill

Each day, hundreds of tourists tramp back up the Avenida do Infante hill to their hotels, unaware that they are passing one of Funchal's most handsome public buildings. Situated approximately one hundred yards up the hill (on the right) after the roundabout, the *Hospício da Princesa* was built in 1859 as a hospital for tuberculosis patients. It was founded in honour of Princess Maria Amelia, daughter of the Brazilian emperor, Pedro I, who died tragically young from tuberculosis. Two fierce-looking dragon trees guard the entrance to lovely shady gardens, which open onto a gleaming white frontage with cheery red doors and shutters.

Walk around the back of the hospital; from here you can see the formidable *Fortaleza do Pico*, constructed between the late 16th and mid-17th centuries. Now isolated from the bay by high-rise buildings, it is used as a navy radio station. There is no public access.

During his time as governor, Zarco is thought to have lived just a few yards farther uphill in the **Quinta das Cruzes**. Originally built in the 15th century, but rebuilt after an earthquake in 1748 and added to in the 19th century, this is Funchal's finest *quinta* open to the public. The main house is now a museum of antiques, including furniture from a variety of centuries and origins, amongst which you will find 16th-century Indo-Portuguese and 17th-century Madeiran as well as 18th- and 19th-century English pieces.

The house is surrounded by a lovely garden in which there are many exotic flowers, trees, and plants (including a good orchid section). However, the outstanding feature is the "archaeological garden," an outdoor display of relics from some of the oldest places on the island—tombstones, pieces taken from important buildings, and two splendid stone Manueline windows (pick up the Quinta's own leaflet for information on these).

The road separating Quinta das Cruzes from the Convento leads to a lookout point with a view over the town, the port, and the dome of the English Church.

## ☞ The Market, Old Town, and Seafront

Walk alongside the cathedral, past the ever-present, much-photographed flower sellers, and along Rua Aljube into Rua Dr. Fernão Ornelas, where there are plenty of intriguing old shops to discover. Rua Ornelas spans two of the capital's *ribeiras* (riverbeds) that carry excess water down from the mountains to the sea. These are also used for sewage purposes, so it is not advisable to linger for too long. In spite of the uncertain aroma, however, the little rivers do make a surprisingly pretty picture, hidden beneath trellises of blazing

> **Signs: entrada –** entrance / **saída –** exit, **chengada –** arrival / **partida –** departure.

bougainvillaea. Just before you cross the Ribeira de João Gomes you will see yet more flower sellers forming their own mini-market.

Directly ahead lies the **Mercado dos Lavradores** (Workers' Market), which is housed in a two-storey, open-roofed structure built in 1941. The market is open from Monday to Saturday; the best time to visit is on a Friday or Saturday, when farmers and traders from all over the island pour into town to ply their wares. This is the only time when the central part is filled with stalls.

*Selling flowers not only attracts tourists, but is a flourishing business in Funchal.*

The whole market is an assault on the senses: noisy, fragrant, colourful, and exotic, with strange fruits, vegetables, and fish of all shapes, colours, and sizes. There are meat stalls around the outside, as well as several wicker and handicraft shops. You will also find an open-air fruit, vegetable, and clothes market just behind the main market, in the park area next to the bus stops.

This is actually the start of the **Old Town** quarter (even though you will not see *Zona Velha* signs until farther east), with the main streets being the narrow, cobbled alleyway of Rua de Santa Maria and, parallel, Rua Dom Carlos I. This east end of Funchal is the antithesis of the opulent Hotel Zone to the west, yet, poor and decaying as it is, it is also filled with character. The only gentrification that has oc-

*The Chapel of Corpo Santo has kept the religious spirit strong for five hundred years.*

curred is to the row of restaurants that you reach at the pedestrianized stretch of cobbled street leading to the **Chapel of Corpo Santo**. The chapel, built at the end of the 15th century, is the oldest in Funchal. Although a few artisan's workshops are to be found close by, this old fishermen's quarter is mainly a residential area. Wind your way along a narrow alleyway, past Edwardian-style beach huts which local fishermen use for storage and napping in, and you will arrive at the 17th-century Forte de São Tiago. As part of an ongoing renovation project, this picturesque fort now houses a Museum of Modern Art. Another sign that this part of Funchal is being revitalized is the new lido, known as Barreirinha, on the beach below the Igreja de Santa Maria Maior. This elegant 18th-century church is well with a visit, and you can take a coffee-break on the terrace of the café below, from where you'll enjoy fine views of the sea to the east.

Walk back to town along the seafront and cross the road at **Parliament House**. Built in the 16th century and formerly the Old Customs House (Alfândega Velha), you can see the oldest parts of this building by stepping inside the rather intimidating gateway, where an official might beckon you into a stone-paved lobby area. This is dominated by an enormous vase decorated in Egyptian style, which at 5.34 metres (17 feet 6 inches) tall, stands almost as high as a giraffe. Made recently by a team of Portuguese and Brazilian craftsmen, it has been given an entry in the *Guinness Book of Records* for being the world's tallest ceramic vase.

Another equally bizarre fact is that the handsome boat that is now the Vagrante Restaurant, moored almost opposite Parliament House in permanent dry dock, once belonged to Liverpool's own John, Paul, George, and Ringo, and is still known as "The Beatles Boat."

## West of Town

Avenida Arriaga finishes at the Praça do Infante, where a statue of Prince Henry the Navigator (a copy of the one at Lagos in the Algarve) sits at the easternmost tip of **Santa Catarina Park**. This is a delightful hilltop retreat, offering respite from the thunderously busy Avenida do Infante and, on the opposite side, splendid views over the Marina to the bay beyond. Aside from the gardens, lake, and playground, other points of interest include the statue of Christopher Columbus (who may have lived in Funchal for a while), and, close by, the Chapel of Santa Catarina, dating from the 17th century. At the west end of the park, the elegant pink **Quinta Vigia** (also known as Quinta Angústias) is the residence of Madeira's governor. The well-tended gardens are open to the public, as is the chapel.

Above the park looms the startling sight of the Casino Park Hotel (designed by Oscar Niemeyer, famous for his thoroughly modern Brasilia). Even the holiday brochures admit that this is less than an esthetic delight, but the facilities inside justify the 5-star rating. The Casino Park signals the start of the **Hotel Zone**. Here you will find more luxury 5-star hotels, such as the Savoy, the Madeira Carlton, and the famous Reid's, plus a few 4-star hotels, *quintas,* and posh restaurants, all offering top-of-the-range Madeiran hospitality.

*Quinta Magnolia Park in the late afternoon—a fine place in which to while away time and watch passersby.*

Also in this area is delightful **Quinta Magnolia Park**, a few yards up Rua Dr. Pita, off Avenida do Infante. Here you can swim or play tennis in the morning, enjoy lunch in the Hotel School restaurant, where dishes are prepared and served by senior students (see page 134), have a walk round the gardens, and round off the afternoon with tea on the patio.

Just west of Reid's Hotel is another hotel zone known as the **Tourist Zone**. Here, too, you will find quality accommodation, a good supermarket, first-class fish restaurants, and an excellent lido (see page 76). At present, however, the Tourist Zone has the haphazard look of a building site about it, with tracts of open ground still awaiting the complete overhaul and subsequent development that will transform such areas into sorely-needed parkland.

## Glorious Gardens

A short bus ride into the steep hillsides northeast of Funchal will bring you to the **Jardim Botânico** (Botanical Garden), the island's most comprehensive public garden. You'll find almost every plant that grows on Madeira here, arranged in steep terraces which offer fine views over Funchal. There's also a small museum, which is similar in both style and content to the Museu Municipal in town (see page 29).

You will find two other attractions nearby: the adjacent **Jardim dos Loiros** (Tropical Bird Gardens), and just a short walk down the hill, **Jardim Orquídea** (Orchid Garden). The Bird Gardens don't really live up to their name. Despite an interesting collection of birds, the manner in which they are displayed—along bare concrete walkways—is totally uninspired. The Jardim Orquídea, meanwhile, is a totally new project in orchid breeding and as yet cannot compete with the displays and mature gardens of its nearest rival, **Quinta da Boa Vista**. You'll need to get a taxi to see that lovely 200-year

*At the Jardim Botânico you'll find a little bit of everything that blooms on the island.*

old house and garden set above Funchal (5 minutes by car), but it's worth the trouble. The focal point of the collection is the orchid display, renowned for its cymbidiums. These have received many awards, most notably from the British Royal Horticultural Society. Orchids are also on sale here, and you will never find them any fresher. Don't leave without wandering around the grounds, which include an ancient wine press and a charming thatched cottage.

For most visitors, however, best of all Madeira's horticultural wonders are the splendid **Palheiro Gardens** (formerly called the Blandy Gardens), which at 550 metres (1,800 feet) are set higher, but are still only a short bus ride from Funchal. The Quinta do Palheiro was the original *quinta* and chapel of the Count of Carvahal, but it has been in the hands of the Blandy family for more than a century. (Adam and Christina Blandy now live here, but their house is closed to the public.)

The gardens, established over several generations, are most famous for their camellias, though there is something here for everyone with green fingers. The long, cobbled entrance avenue, for instance, is shaded by plane trees, while the fields which lie on each side are carpeted with a wonderful spread of agapanthus and arum and belladonna lilies in season.

Exotic plants, amongst them a lush array of tropical species, are a constant source of intrigue and interest. Formal and informal areas provide a variety of styles, with pools and fountains, and landscaped terraces roll gently down the hillsides. Despite these touches, however, the garden has managed to retain the distinctive charming and peaceful atmosphere of the timeless grounds of an English country house.

*Lush greenery and colourful gardens surround the elegant Quinta do Palheiro.*

## AROUND FUNCHAL

Tour operators combine the delights of Monte, Pico dos Barcelos, and Curral das Freiras to make up a popular half-day excursion; if you are doing it under your own steam, allow a full day so you can visit the Monte Palace Gardens and make the most of a leisurely lunch.

**Monte** (meaning "mount") has been a fashionable hill-town above Funchal ever since wealthy merchants and exiled European aristocrats decided in the 19th century to build their splendid *quintas* up here in the fresh cool air.

The square in Monte, where taxis and coaches set down, recalls the good old days when the area was at its peak. The railway station is still here; the arches over the perfectly clipped **Old Monte Gardens** (established 1894) once carried the rack-and-pinion railway that laboured up the ferociously steep hill. Sadly, in 1930, after some 37 years' service, the train blew up and a number of people were killed. The railway stopped running and then, with the advent of World War II, Monte's golden age was over.

A short walk up from the square is the elegant and richly decorated **Igreja de Nossa Senhora do Monte** (Our Lady of Monte), dedicated to Madeira's patron saint. On 15 August, thousands of locals make the annual pilgrimage to this place. A chapel on the left holds the tomb of the last of the Austro-Hungarian emperors, Charles I of Austria (and IV of Hungary), who died on Madeira in 1922. The church is also the starting point for the island's best-known attraction, the unique roller-coaster ride down the hill aboard a wicker toboggan (see page 42).

Monte's newest attraction, the **Monte Palace Tropical Gardens**, is also firmly rooted in the past. The glorious gardens that surround the beautiful, château-like Monte Palace

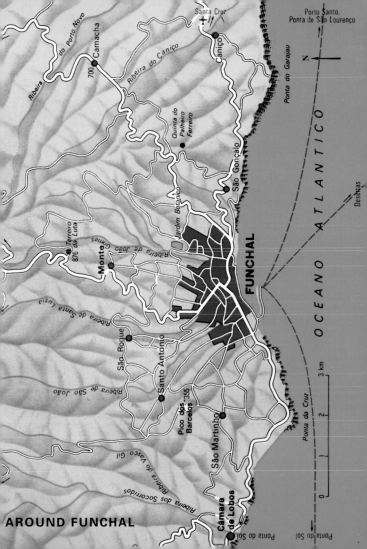

**AROUND FUNCHAL**

—once the area's most fashionable hotel—are now home to hundreds of plants and various other displays. The entrance fee is high by Madeiran standards (1,000 escudos), but within you will discover an impressive collection of native and exotic flora (especially good cycads), a koi pond, a fine porcelain collection, historical artefacts from throughout Portugal, in-

## Downhill Racers

*Carros de cestos*, the famous Madeiran toboggans, were originally used at the beginning of the 19th century to carry freight down the frighteningly steep 5 km (3 mile) hill between Monte and Funchal. It is said that it was a British merchant, living on the hill and fed up with winding his weary way down to Funchal every day, who hit on the idea that the same toboggans could carry people. A wicker seat was fixed to the basic sled and so the *carro de cesto* (literally "basket-car") was born.

In order to avoid the perils of a headlong plunge into oblivion, each *carro* is controlled by two white-attired *carreiros*, complete with traditional straw hats, who give an initial push and then ride along until another push, or pull, or sudden brake, is required, depending upon the desired speed and any traffic ahead. The *carro de cesto* has for many years been the thing to do in Funchal, and many a cruise-ship passenger has been whisked up to Monte to make the journey, before disappearing almost straight back to sea.

Alas, the current toboggan ride is a pale shadow of its former self. Within the last few years the road surface has been changed from friction-free, slippery cobbles to a sure-gripping asphalt surface. The final result is that the toboggans roll downhill considerably slower than they used to, and the *carreiros* are having to push much harder for their money. However, the lot of the *carreiros* seems to have changed for the better. They used to have to walk back up the hill, carrying or pushing the 68 kg (150 pound) sleds, but nowadays a taxi takes them up and a lorry transports the *carros*.

cluding architectural pieces taken from important buildings and prized *azulejo* panels, as well as Oriental Gardens and a lake with a water-cannon folly. From here, the unimpeded views of Funchal are unbeatable.

**Terreiro da Luta**, at 876 metres (2,873 feet), lies just over 1.5 km (1 mile) north of Monte, but adds an additional 330 metres (1,000 feet) to the altitude (and offers another magnificent panorama of Funchal). It

*A few locals take a rest on the steps of the Igreja de Nossa Senhora de Monte.*

was here that the revered figure of Our Lady of the Mount (now in the church below) was allegedly discovered under miraculous circumstances in the 15th century.

Today on the summit you will find a monument to Our Lady of Peace (Nossa Senhora da Paz), which was dedicated to the end of World War I. Around the monument are anchor chains from French ships sunk in Funchal harbour by German torpedoes.

Yet more views of Funchal and its surroundings can be enjoyed at **Pico dos Barcelos** (along with the souvenir stalls and restaurants). Although at 355 metres (1,164 feet) the altitude of the balcony is less than half that of Terreiro da Luta, the sweeping views from west to east and back into the terraced hillsides are well worth seeing. If you have brought your own transport, make a short detour to see the handsome landmark church of **São Martinho**. It's surprising to find such a large church in a relatively isolated farming parish.

Head north for 16 km (10 miles) on the narrow, twisting road to **Curral das Freiras** and you will discover a village that until very recently was truly isolated from the outside world. The name translates as "Corral of the Nuns," but it is better known as the "Valley of the Nuns" or the "Crater," because of its shape, a circle surrounded by extinct volcanoes. The nuns in question fled here from Santa Clara Convent in the 16th century to escape raiding pirates. Protected on all sides by inaccessible mountains, their settlement became permanent. A mixture of rich volcanic soil and abundant sunshine combined to support the hidden village, and it became famous for its cherries and the popular cherry distillation called *ginja*. The cakes here are also excellent. The village continued in splendid isolation until quite recently, when tunnels were finally bored through the mountains to bring the first roads. The villagers had to wait until 1986 before their first television pictures arrived.

A visit to the village of Curral das Freiras is not, however, the main reason for this trip. It's a pleasant enough place, but in truth there is very little here. The magical part of this excursion is the view from above, down into the valley. The most famous view is from directly above the village at the lookout point of **Eira do Serrado** (1,006 metres/3,300 feet). If you are taking a coach tour, make sure a stop at Eira do Serrado is included. An alternative view is from the south, way across the valley, at the lookout point with the romantic name of **Boca dos Namorados** (Lovers' Nest). This is a difficult trek which, although feasible by car, is also incorporated on the itinerary of jeep safaris. From here, the panorama sweeps round and takes in the entire valley (though even at 3,608 metres/1,100 feet you'll still be close enough to hear the bell of the village church), and immediately conjures up wonderful Alpine images of Austria or Switzerland.

**Camacha**, set at a refreshing altitude of nearly 700 metres (2,300 feet), is in the heart of willow country and, as a result, is famous throughout the island as the heart of the wickerwork industry. Around 2,000 people in the region are involved in this work, making everything from furniture to hats out of wicker. Around Camacha and north of here it is likely that you will see the stripped willow soaked and left to dry, either by a river bank, propped up against a house, or in wigwam fashion in the fields. You may even see families sitting at the roadside, some of whom will probably be cooking the willow in cauldron-like vats, and others who will be laboriously stripping off the bark.

Most of the weaving is done in the home, however, and the only place you are guaranteed to see craftsmen at work is in the slightly dingy basement of the **Café Relógio**. Despite its rather dull appearance and the crowds of people, this three-storey "wicker-superstore" is an excellent place for shopping and refreshments. There is a lively café on the ground floor, and, above, a restaurant serving up good Madeiran fare with the bonus of splendid panoramic views.

Camacha itself is a pretty village which can get quite animated, and is certainly worth taking a few minutes just to browse round. It is also an easy point for two excellent *levada* walks (see page 65), both suitable for people of all ages. One heads westwards to Vale do Paraíso, the other north and east to Eira de Fora.

*Willow left to dry in the fields near Camacha may well end up as a basket.*

# ISLAND FLORA

Madeira has gained numerous nicknames due to its wonderful plant life, such as "the Atlantic's Floating Flower Pot" and "God's Botanical Garden." The latter seems particularly appropriate, as the majority of the flora is exotic (as opposed to native), originating from all parts of the world. Most eyes are taken by orchids, flamingo flowers (*anthurium*), and the colourful, plume-like bird-of-paradise flowers (*strelitzias*).

Even if you feel indifferent about plants and flowers before your trip, by the time you leave you will probably have been converted. If you are here during the Flower Festival (see page 80), you may even become something of an expert.

The spectacle of hibiscus (China), blazing bougainvillaea (Brazil), and bird-of-paradise flowers (South Africa) lasts throughout the year. Delights to look for are as follows:

**Spring**. Jacaranda blossoms forth into a violet cloud above Funchal's Avenida Arriaga, which lasts until June. Elsewhere

on the island, see the painted trumpet (South America), the cockscomb coral tree, and the pastel-petalled franciscea (both from Brazil), flame trees, and the unmistakeable red-hot poker (South Africa), which fires up from May to August and contrasts with the cool white lily.

**Summer-Autumn**. On the hills you will find the pride of Madeira, while the common blue or white African lily provides cheery roadside colour. Bright blue hydrangeas (China and Japan) are a familiar sight, while the delicate petals of the frangipani look hand-painted. In August, cassia flowers produce masses of yellow, lasting for three months. The sunny golden trumpet and stiverbush, two South American varieties, bloom through this period as well. Even when in blossom, the dragon tree (found in the Canary Islands and Madeira alone) is a strange, primitive sight. During September,

*Sparaxis (left); bird of paradise (right); and the flamingo flower (below).*

look for creeping podranea (South Africa) and in the hills, pink and white belladonna lilies.

**Winter**. In winter, the kaffir or lucky bean tree blooms with red flowers, and there are not only daisies, but daisy trees as well. Another curious tree to look out for is the kapok, also known as the silk-cotton tree. Its pink flowers blossom from September to November, and in spring a silky, cotton-wool-like fibre is produced, which is used for stuffing cushions and pillows. Poinsettia, a Christmas favourite, blooms in October and lasts until February or well beyond. The vine variously called golden shower or orange trumpet comes out in December and also lasts until February. Dramatic arum lilies are a common sight from November through to June.

Orchids are in their prime until May. Cymbidiums (Asia) are intensely grown for export, so too are cypripediums (various origins), which are known commonly as lady's-slipper.

*Protea flowers.*

## WEST OF THE ISLAND

Our tour commences 10 km (6 miles) west of Funchal at **Câmara de Lobos** ("lair of the sea-wolves"). The village's  peculiar name refers to the seals that once swam around here. They have long gone, though a colony does still inhabit the waters off the Ilhas Desertas.

Ever since 1950, when Winston Churchill painted this picturesque fishing port, it has been caricatured as an idyllic, old-world fishing village. With gaily-painted boats drawn up on the shore alongside swaying palm trees, a protected, rocky, natural harbour, and an old quarter that rises steeply up to the promontory overlooking the ocean, it certainly looks idyllic. Surprisingly, for such a heavily visited place, the port area has resisted any attempts at gentrification and has a very macho atmosphere. Hard-drinking lo-

*A bird's-eye view over the*
*picturesque fishing port of Câmara de Lobos.*

*All in a day's work for a fisherman in Câmara de Lobos.*

cals down the rather potent *poncha* (sugar-cane brandy, lemon juice, and honey) in shadowy bars, while grizzled old fishermen play cards in berthed boats, awaiting their next trip. You will find no tourist souvenir shop or fishing-museum-type frippery here. This is purely and simply a working port.

In spite of its income from fishing, Câmara de Lobos remains poor, as a walk up the hill amongst the local homes will soon tell you. Before you leave, look in the small, white chapel close to the waterfront—it's an early 15th-century project which was later rebuilt (1723). The far end of the village has been tidied up. A neat little church, pretty bandstand, and a couple of local restaurants look out across a pebbly beach onto Cabo Girão.

As you enter from the direction of Funchal, the terrace from where Churchill painted is just above the port. Nowadays, however, the best view of Câmara de Lobos is from the (low-level) *miradouro*, a few hundred yards back towards Funchal. This may involve turning around, as it is easy to miss it on a first visit. If you want a good view of the village, drive to Pico da Torre.

Beyond Câmara de Lobos, the road climbs for some 10 km (6 miles), passing through some of the richest agricultural country in southern Madeira, famous for the high quality of its grapes. Eventually it leads to the top of the mighty headland known as **Cabo Girão**. This is one of the highest sea cliffs in the world, with a drop of 590 metres (1,900 feet) into the Atlantic from the railing at the very end of the cape. Blue and white *agapanthus* cling to the top of the promontory, and pine and eucalyptus grow right to the edge, but an even greater degree of tenacity can be seen hundreds of feet below, where farmers have managed to salvage tiny plots of arable land, terracing them into little green postage stamps stuck onto the sides and base of the cliff.

The winding road continues on through the sprawling settlements of Quinta Grande and Campanário. The latter, an important grape-growing area, is also remarkable for its cliff-side caves, used by local fisher-

*The landmark church of Ribeira Brava is a familiar sight to people from all over the island.*

man for storage purposes. You will need to take a boat trip to see these.

The next major settlement, heading westwards, is **Ribeira Brava**. Its name, which means "wild river" or "ravine," seems inappropriate for such a neat and peaceful little community. You will only see the town's "wild river" in winter, since at other times it's more of a tame trickle. The river heads due north and so does the road (to São Vicente), thus making the town of Ribeira Brava an important junction between the south and north coasts. There are a couple of hotels here and a pleasant stoney beach with umbrellas alongside the Água Mar restaurant.

A tidy square, paved with black, egg-shaped stones from the beach, is the main focus of attention. Next to here lies the small municipal market, while behind is the town centre, with an attractive old church featuring a steeple of blue-and-white tiles.

From Ribeira Brava, many coach excursions head northwards, as this road is one of the most attractive stretches on the whole island, and there are various points of interest *en route*. We will return this way, but if time is limited, then go north to São Vicente (see page 55) and leave out the following south-coast settlements.

**Ponta do Sol** is the next village you will come to. As its name ("sunny point") suggests, it is blessed with more than its fair share of sunshine. Only during the summer does it really come alive, however, when beach umbrellas are set out on the pebbly shore across from the small square. There are two buildings of note here: one is the 18th-century church, which is worth visiting, while the other is the Art-Deco Cinema. As is frequently the case in Madeiran villages, the best views are from vantage points on the hillside road as it climbs up away from the village.

Carry on through Canhas, which is notable for its statue of Santa Teresa and the Stations of the Cross, and some 10 km (6 miles) out of Ponta do Sol there is a *miradouro* overlooking the tiny settlement of Madalena do Mar.

**Calheta**, the next town of significance as you head west, is a banana plantations centre. The parish church, rebuilt in 1639, features a Moorish-style ceiling. Returning to the main road, head back towards Funchal, and after 0.5 km (quarter of a mile) turn left, inland.

After 10 km (6 miles) you will rejoin the main road

*Porto Moniz spills out into the ocean—don't forget your swimming gear if the weather is good.*

linking Paúl da Serra to Porto Moniz. Before turning right towards Porto Moniz, though, it's worth making a short detour by going east (turn right) then almost immediately north (turn left) to pick up a minor road to **Rabaçal**, a beautiful valley that is popular among Madeirans at weekends and on holidays (as indicated by the barbecue facilities). From here there is an easy, short, recommended *levada* walk (about 30 minutes return) to the popular beauty spot of Risco waterfall.

Return to the main road and continue west. **Paúl da Serra** ("marsh of the mountains") is the only plateau on the island and measures around 16 square km (6 square miles). The scenery and landscape here are reminiscent of the bleak moors of Scotland, but if the weather is good the plateau still attracts hikers, precisely because of its remote and barren character, which is so different from the rest of the island. If you are thinking of walking or hiking here, be warned that mists descend suddenly, and you may want to go with a guide.

**Porto Moniz**, located 70 km (44 miles) from Funchal on the northwest tip of the island, is journey's end. This is a small place, with few facilities other than a couple of hotels and restaurants (which welcome coach parties). There's a great view from the hill above. The village's tiny fields are walled off into small boxes by heath-tree fencing (to protect crops from the salt-laden wind), and a volcanic extension (something of an afterthought of a peninsula) reaches out into the Atlantic. The reefs here form natural pools, and with a few chunks of concrete thrown in to fill some crucial gaps, an attractive, semi-natural lido has taken shape.

East from here, the coast road is an attraction in itself. In some places it hugs the coastline, then climbs up the mountainside, clinging precariously to a narrow ledge. Look out for the rocky outcrop with a hole—like an open window, the shape of which has lent itself to the name of the nearest settlement, Ribeira da Janela (River of the Window). Water rushes down from the mountains here at a tremendous rate; some is employed in hydro-electricity stations, but a lot simply drains off into the sea, splashing off car roofs en route (convertible drivers beware!).

**Seixal** (Sayshall) is the only other settlement between here and São Vicente. A pretty village at the centre of a wine-growing district, it is the place after which the Sercial grape (which is used to produce the driest style of Madeira) takes its name. Outside Seixal, heading east, it is well worth taking a short detour to make the steep climb up to the beauty spot of **Chão da Ribeira**.

The village of **São Vicente** begins at the point where the coastal road meets the north-south road heading 21 km (13 miles) to Ribeira Brava. An unusual small chapel has been hollowed out of a rock, though if heading south you may not catch sight of it without looking back. A couple of restaurants and an *estalagem* (inn) are on the front, but the village itself is set a little inland, away from the harsh ocean winds.

São Vicente is probably the prettiest village on the island, and is unlike many of the others in that it is compact, well cared for, and enjoys the great bonus of being pedestrianized. Tourism is making itself felt here, and cafés and restaurants have been designed with trippers in mind, but no one could say the village has been spoilt. It also boasts a lovely church with a colourful interior that includes a painted ceiling depicting both São Vicente and, of course, the church itself.

*The roofscape of São Vicente — Madeira's best-kept secret and a favourite place for a day trip.*

High on a hill above the village is a strange church—actually a clockless clock tower—standing over a small chapel dedicated to Our Lady of Fátima. This isolated spot is a significant pilgrimage place, and can be seen for miles around. The road continues to cut its way through beautiful, verdant countryside until finally coming to a crest at the pass of **Boca da Encumeada** (626 metres/1,007 feet). From this point you can see right to the north coast and well into the south, while stretching on each side are vast expanses of mountain scenery, which will give you some idea of the island's geological and topographical make-up.

Just a few miles south of the pass you will find the most attractively positioned mountain accommodation on Madeira, the **Pousada dos Vinháticos** (*vinhático* is a type of Madeiran mahogany tree). This government-run establishment, something akin to a mountain chalet, enjoys the sort of

*Two different terraces—one for growing crops, the other for enjoying the view and drinking tea.*

views that many Alpine hotels would cherish. It's the perfect place for tea on the terrace, but don't expect to find solitude here, as this is a busy stopping point for excursions.

The valley on the opposite side of the road and south of the *pousada* is known as **Serra de Água**, and lays claim to the distinction of being the island's first hydro-electric power station. In spite of the introduction of modern technology, however, the valley's lush hills resemble more the Garden of Eden than an industrialized landscape.

The road leads down into Ribeira Brava, from where a new motorway allows you to make a quick trip back to Funchal in 20 minutes.

## EAST OF THE ISLAND

The road east from Funchal winds past some of the town's smartest villas. The first landmark you'll see is the church of São Gonçalo in the parish of the same name. Just below, the A Montanha restaurant enjoys a super view looking west over Funchal harbour. Also to be found in the vicinity is the tiny, atmospheric chapel dedicated to Nossa Senhora das Neves (Our Lady of the Snows).

After roughly another mile, turn off the main road towards **Garajau**, where a recent holiday development has proven very popular with German visitors. The road ends at a fine *miradouro*, where a Statue of Christ stands with arms outstretched (a miniature version of the statues at Rio de Janeiro and Lisbon). Here, also, you get a good view west to the Bay of Funchal; to the east, the modern resort on the small promontory is Caniço de Baixa, another favourite with German holidaymakers.

Look down to see a settlement of a very different nature. It is doubtful whether the accumulative value of the collection of ramshackle huts and houses which now constitute

*Cliff-top holiday homes on the Caniço de Baixa are privy to splendid ocean views.*

old Garajau would buy even a single villa out on popular Caniço de Baixa.

To continue back to the main road: the first settlement of any real size is **Caniço**. The original village is built around an imposing 18th-century church, while the new Caniço de Baixa is a sprawling proliferation of smart holiday homes visible from afar.

These days Santa Cruz is known for its international airport. What you might not have realized when landing, though, is its tiny size. Viewed from a distance, it is not dissimilar to an aircraft carrier (the runway itself is being extended, with a completion date in 1999). As you continue driving east, you actually travel underneath the runway, which is supported on huge pillars above you—a novel (not to mention rather sobering) sensation both for those above and below.

The town of **Santa Cruz** is a pleasant place, with an attractive church dating from the 16th century. Across the main square, the town hall, in spite of having been modernized, retains a pair of splendid 15th- to 16th-century Manueline windows. A few streets away, the courthouse is another survivor of that era, with fine verandahs and an impressive main staircase. Along the seafront is the modern municipal market and a pebbly beach. A new cultural center schedules events throughout the year. Roughly 2 km (just over a mile) farther west, the small, modern complex of holiday apartments at Matur gives way to Machico. For a fine view over the town and its large bay, the road climbs up to a *miradouro*.

**Machico** can claim to be Madeira's first settlement, as this is where João Gonçalves Zarco first came ashore on the island in 1419. His fellow Portuguese captain and navigator, Tristão Vaz Teixeira, ruled the eastern half of the island from Machico. A statue of Teixeira stands outside the town's 15th-century parish church. King Manuel I donated the statue of

*Life in Machico is as traditional as ever.*

the Virgin (over the altar) and the distinguished church portal. The latter is a fine example of the exuberant style of architecture named after him.

From Machico's triangular "square," several streets lead to the seafront. Facing the beach is a small fort with an inscription dated 1706. Although of a similar style to Funchal's twin defences, it is not as daunting. A few yards to the left is a pleasant restaurant-café. Continue walking along the front until you get to the river. The local fishermen's quarters lie to the east of here. Unless the river is raging, you will probably see cows grazing along the banks, a scene more similar to a Constable painting than sub-tropical Madeira, where cows are usually confined to tiny huts.

Machico is one of Madeira's boat-building centres, and on the beach you will probably see work in progress on both old and new vessels, with the former being used for scrap. Large, new tuna boats are currently being built (with the aid of EU funding) to replace old stock. Follow the road all the way round the bay for a fine view across, from east to west. The incongruous high-rise blot on the landscape directly opposite is the Hotel Dom Pedro, signalling the tourism ambitions of the town.

The road heads inland after Machico, into a long, dark tunnel before the fishing village of Caniçal heaves into view. Before that, however, you will find a huge, fenced-off area under construction as a *zona franca*—tax-free business development area—intended to attract foreign investment. With so little in the way of industrial development elsewhere on the island, this Colditz-like zone is particularly startling.

The landscape of the eastern peninsula, known as the **Ponta de São Lourenço**, is more like Porto Santo and the Ilhas Desertas than Madeira. It is wild and windswept, and its limited vegetation is a far cry from the lush green interior. Keen walkers enjoy this tip of the island, but for many it is a little too invigorating for comfort.

**Caniçal** was once a famous whaling port, but since whaling was banned in these waters in 1981, all that remains of this formerly lucrative industry is a Museum of Whaling and a few scrimshaw and whalebone souvenirs in a hut by the beach (more of the same is on sale at the car park at the end of the road heading east).

Although the **Whale Museum** (Museu da Baleia) shows a video of a whale hunt in 1978, the owner, Senhor Reis, is the epitome of a poacher turned gamekeeper. Once commander of the Caniçal whaling station and thus responsible for taking 100-200 of these great creatures each year, he now devotes his energy to saving the whale and other marine life of the area. The 14-metre- (45-foot-) long model of the sperm whale is a reminder of the leviathans that once swam in great schools in the waters of Madeira. Whales are still sighted here, but no longer frequently.

The beach of Caniçal now looks rather forlorn, with rotting hulks and flotsam and jetsam testifying to better days. Nevertheless, this is a working fishing port, complete with a selection of good fish restaurants. Close by, at Prainha, is the island's only natural sandy beach. Not surprisingly for a volcanic island, the sand here is black, and even this stretch is sometimes washed away.

To continue on your eastern tour of the island, you have to backtrack to Machico and turn north along the road following the Ribeira de Machico. Stop off at **Portela**; there's a good restaurant here, and at 662 metres (2,172 feet) this point offers fine views of both north and south coasts and the **Penha d'Águia** which dominates the northeast coast. This huge rock formation, towering at 590 metres (1,935 feet),

*Classic palheiro house in Santana; some are no
longer inhabited, others are tiny homes.*

levels off to a flat top. The name, meaning Eagle Rock, is de-
rived from its former inhabitants rather than its shape.

The village of Porto da Cruz, 6 km (4 miles) north, lies in
the shadow of the rock. Here you will find one of Madeira's
few sugarcane mills still working, pumping out steam as it
processes the sugarcane to make *aguardente*, the local
liquor. It doesn't operate all year round, however, and it is
open to the public only in April. The village is neat and tidy,
but there's nothing to detain you very long.

Just to the north of here lies **Faial**, much photographed because of its picturesque setting right at the foot of the Penha
d'Águia. There is little of note in the village itself, aside from
its handsome church and the Casa de Chá do Faial, which de-

spite its name (Tearooms of Faial) is a standard restaurant with picture windows and fine roof-top panoramas.

The road winds westwards on its way up and out of the village, where there are at least two memorable lookout points looking back towards the east from the main road. If you have been around the island for a few days, you will probably have noticed either postcards or miniature replicas of the A-shaped houses known as *palheiros* (not be confused with the A-shaped cow huts which dot the hillsides all over Madeira). The classic *palheiro* is white stucco with a brightly painted red door, red and blue window frames and shutters, and above all, a thatched roof. The only village where this picturesque but primitive style of housing can still be found is **Santana**.

In no way is this a classical, compact village, solely made up of such fairy-tale houses. In fact, it's a rather straggly place with a very modern town hall and no identifiable centre. Two *palheiros*, perfectly painted in red, white, and blue, stand nearby (though they are uninhabited, locked, and only for the tourist gaze), while a third one functions as a public toilet. You will find an inhabited *palheiro* just behind these.

Elsewhere, there are miniature *palheiro* dog kennels, and down by the river even the ducks have their own *palheiro*. The rest of the village is, for the most part, modern and ordinary, with the odd traditional *palheiro* dotted here and there. If you want to take a look inside one, there is also a furnished "showhouse" *palheiro* next to the O Colmo restaurant, where you can see the extremely confined living space.

More thatched houses of a larger and more conventional kind are to be found 5 km (3 miles) south of Santana. The government-owned **Casa das Queimadas** is a complex of cottage-style rest houses with attractive gardens. It's a lovely spot for a picnic, although if the weather is clear you might prefer to take the opportunity to ascend to the very top of the island. This is reached by a 10 km (6 mile) drive south of Santana, through the forest park of Pico das Pedras, up to **Achada do Teixeira** at 1,592 metres (5,223 feet). From here, it's a 2-hour (return) walk to Pico Ruivo, at 1,862 metres (6,109 feet) the highest point on Madeira (see page 67).

The scenery north of Santana is every bit as good as it was south of the village. **São Jorge** boasts a fine, richly ornamented church, while past the village there is a splendid panorama from the *miradouro* of **Cabanas**, over to the valley of Arco de São Jorge. *Cabanas* means cabins, and the small, disused, circular *cabanas* here bear testimony to a tourist-village scheme that was meant to transform the area but never made it off the ground.

The road winds inland towards the picturesque, fertile countryside in the vicinity of Faja do Penedo and on to the pretty village of Boaventura. Follow the coast road to enjoy excellent views down to the small peninsula of **Ponta Delgada**, where you can cool off by the rocks in the seawater swimming pool. From here it's just 5 km (3 miles) to São Vicente, at which point the road heads south to Ribeira Brava, then east back to Funchal.

## MADEIRA'S MOUNTAINS

The rugged mountain chain splitting the island into north and south makes weather forecasting a pretty unrewarding occupation on Madeira. While it is usually warm and clear down in Funchal, the mountains are often shrouded in a wintry mist. However, all is not lost if this is the case, since the tops of the mountains may be jutting through the clouds, and while your views will not be unimpeded, the spectacle of these majestic peaks above the cotton-wool layers is something to behold in itself. Unfortunately, however, you are un-likely to know that until you get up there. The best advice is, if it looks clear, beat a hasty path up to Pico do Arieiro—first thing in the morning is usually the best time, although there is no guaranteee. There is also a much better chance of clear mountain tops in summer than during the rest of the year. If the weather isn't clear but the clouds are coming low into Funchal, then travel hopefully. You should know by the time you arrive at Poiso whether or not your journey is worth the effort. If it's raining, console yourself that it's only a 23 km (14 mile) drive from Funchal, and you can always try again the next day.

## Levadas

*Levadas* are simply irrigation channels that are cut no more than a few inches wide, and set a foot or two into the ground. Running for more than 2,150 km (1,300 miles) all around Madeira, they have been here for almost as long as the island has been settled.

The footpaths alongside each *levada* were built for maintenance purposes, but also provide a great network on which to explore the interior of the island. In fact, many people come to Madeira just for the walking. Some *levadas* are suitable for all ages; the only requirements are reasonable footwear and possibly a taxi waiting at the other end. As most *levadas* wind around the hillsides, gradients usually remain gentle. Nonetheless, paths that follow the lie of the hillside can also give rise to unexpected vertiginous drops.

To get to grips with the walks, try to find a copy of *Landscapes of Madeira* by John and Pat Underwood, sold in many local bookstores.

At 1,800 metres (5,900 feet), **Pico do Arieiro** may only be the second-highest peak on Madeira, but it is the highest point which can be reached by car and is therefore a popular destination. As the road rises, the rugged countryside becomes more spectacular, with plunging volcanic hillsides softened and greened by time. If you're driving, beware of sheep straying onto the road above Poiso.

The lookout point at the summit provides a 360-degree **panorama**. With its stratified canyon walls, a field of frozen lava, and boulders flung across the scene of volcanic catastrophe, it's a geologist's dream. During summer, the terrain is parched, while at other times of the year it's often covered with snow. The overnight temperature plunges below freezing most of the year, while the average annual temperature is less than 10°C (50°F). There is also six

*The rolling countryside on the way to Pico do Arieiro.*

times as much rain here as in Funchal. If the arrival of clouds catches you unawares, you can always sit it out in the modern but warm and welcoming *pousada*.

**Pico Ruivo**, at the very top of Madeira, lies only another 62 metres (209 feet) higher than Pico do Arieiro, but is harder to get to. Access to the peak is via either a 60-minute walk from the north, from Achada do Teixeira (see page 64), or the classic, but rather more strenuous, 4-hour, roof-of-the-island hike (2 hours there, 2 hours back) from Pico do Arieiro. The latter is well signposted and there is a paved footpath, with drops protected by railings.

On a good day you will see several other walkers, so don't worry about losing your way (or getting lonely). Take warm clothing and sturdy footwear, though, and in winter bear in mind that conditions on the mountains can be hazardous, with landslides removing parts of the path. Check the weather conditions from the tourist information office in Funchal, then double-check at the *pousada* when you get there.

Having come by car from Funchal, you will have passed through Poiso, which is simply a crossroads restaurant as far as most tourists are concerned. Return to there and then head on towards **Ribeiro Frio**. The name means "cold river," and will give you an idea of what sort of weather to expect out of summer. There is something of a cool micro-climate here, and the dominant building, Victor's Bar (also a good restaurant), rather appropriately resembles an Alpine chalet. If the change in climate is too much, you'll appreciate the warm, pub-like interior with its log fires, compared by some visitors to a Kenyan mountain lodge.

Adjacent to the restaurant is a tiny chapel, a government trout hatchery, a small botanical garden, and a couple of shops. The trout hatchery is a series of small, interconnected concrete pools, where the trout become increasingly bigger as you go along the pools. (The tastiest of these will end up on the menu at Victor's Bar.) The botanical garden is not in the same league as the beautiful gardens you will see in Funchal, but it nevertheless claims to perpetuate every species of flower, plant, and tree to be found on Madeira, and sprawls unpredictably along twisting paths among shady trees.

You can see all that Ribeiro Frio has to offer in just a few minutes, but two **walks** which start from here are the principal attraction of the place. The shorter, 2 km (1 mile) walk to the lookout point known as the **Balcões** (meaning "balconies") takes just 45 minutes return (round-trip), and is rewarded by views into the heart of the island, across steep hillsides and dramatic ravines to the distinctive peaks of Ruivo and Arieiro.

The second walk is one of the island's most popular *levada* trails and continues for just over 10 km (6 miles) until it reaches Portela, where a good restaurant offers sustenance to weary hikers. The walk will take between three and four hours, so you may wish to arrange for a taxi to collect you at Portela. An alternative short walk is to head out along the *levada* for 20 minutes or so (before the steep drops start to occur), by which time you will certainly have been able to sample its charm, and then head back to Ribeiro Frio. Whichever of the options you choose, you know there will be food and drink waiting at the end!

As you head out of Funchal, the village of **Santo da Serra** can also be reached via Camacha or from the Poiso crossroads. The name is an abbreviation of Santo Antonio da Serra. The altitude of 670 metres (2,200 feet) ensures refreshing breezes, and explains why wealthy British residents chose to build their *quintas* here, as well as why so many affluent Madeirans still flee the hot Funchal summer up into these hills.

The most striking feature of Santo da Serra is its flatness; it may not be a large plateau in the league of Paúl da Serra, but it is still big enough to accommodate a 27-hole golf course. Even if you're not much of a golfer, you might still enjoy a stroll through the pleasant gardens of **Quinta da Junta** park, which was once owned by the Blandy family but is now public. A lookout point provides views across to Machico on the coast, and you can enjoy a drink at the golf club bar, set in what was once a *pousada*.

## PORTO SANTO

The island of Porto Santo, 40 km (25 miles) northeast of Madeira, is the only other inhabited island in the archipelago, with a population of some 5,000. As desert islands go, it's not exactly undiscovered, but only a handful of foreign visitors find these shores, and Porto Santo is still at heart the resort of the Madeirans.

One glance at the long, golden, sandy beach, scarcely touched by development, will tell you why—there's nothing remotely like this on the main island. Beach aside, you may be

---

### False Prophets, Magical Sands

The inhabitants of Porto Santo are sometimes referred to by Madeirans as *profetas,* meaning prophets, as the result of a strange episode in the 16th century, when a local shepherd started a religious cult. Not only did he say he could predict the future, but he held people in sway by claiming the power to list their most intimate secrets and sins. Fortunately, the cult was short-lived and the *Portosantenses* resumed normality.

Magical powers of a different kind are also attributed to the island's beach, for it is said to hold curative properties which alleviate all kinds of aches and pains. Many Madeirans and locals are convinced of its benefits.

*The Church of Our Lady of Piety is the glowing centre-piece of the tiny town of Vila Baleira.*

surprised by how different Porto Santo looks compared to Madeira. In summer it is, on the whole, scorched and yellow; its rusty-coloured rock and cliff formations have led to its being dubbed "the tawny island." It's mostly quiet, with a short, three-month summer season, when, quite unbelievably, several discotheques open their doors to compete for trade. Out of season, however, even the main town seems deserted.

If you have opted for the sea crossing, you will step ashore at Porto de Abrigo on the eastern tip of the island. You may be quite glad to see terra firma, as the crossing can be very rough (but usually only out of season). The return crossing, however, is never as bad. From the dock it is a short taxi or bus ride, or a 15- to 20-minute walk, to Vila Baleira (sometimes referred to as Porto Santo Town), the island's one and only settlement of notable size.

The centre of **Vila Baleira** is a small, triangular "square," comprising a correspondingly small town hall and a church which has been recently restored after more than three centuries of use. Nossa Senhora da Piedade (Our Lady of Piety) was originally founded just after the island's discovery during the early to middle-15th century. The present church was rebuilt after pirates destroyed the original in 1667, though part of it, the Morgada chapel, did survive.

The town's major attraction is the house that stands next to the church, set back a little off the square. **Casa de Colombo** (closed weekends) dates from the 15th century as well and, like its neighbour, has recently been restored. It's an atmospheric place built from rough-hewn stone, and you can easily imagine Christopher Columbus staying here. There is no doubt that Columbus was on the island, for he married Felipa Moniz Perestrelo, daughter of the first Governor of Porto Santo, Bartolomeu Perestrelo; but there is no strong evidence that he ever lived here. The museum, however, claims that around 1480, Senhor and Senhora Colombo lived here for about two years, and young Diego Columbo was born a *Portosantense* in this house.

Whatever the truth may be—and there is no strong historical evidence either way—the Casa de Colombo is worth a visit. Displays include period pieces, memorabilia, replicas, maps, paintings, and sketches, but there is nothing directly linked with the man himself. Another curious enigma about Columbus is that no reliable likeness of him has ever survived. Take a look at the portraits in the museum, and then compare them with the dashing, modern bust of him in the public gardens by the quay. (While you're at the quay, also take a look at at the abstract memorial to the Discoverers, which has so far failed to win wide praise from either visitors or locals.)

On the way to the gardens, go to the tourist office, where friendly staff will assist you with leaflets and information, as

well as showing you a video of the island. The most interesting street in Vila Baleira is Rua João Gonçalves Zarco, just
the other side of the river, running down to the sea. Here you
will find the town's small market and a number of old shops
and bars that are full of character.

## An Island Tour

It seems scarcely worthwhile renting a car on Porto Santo, as
the island measures less than 11 km by 6 km (7 miles by 4
miles) at its widest points and in total covers only 41 sq km
(16 sq miles). Hiring a car is expensive, there is not much to
see, and what there is to see is usually off the main roads.
Taxis will take you around the island, giving their own tours
at fixed prices (see page 124), so there is no risk of your being
cheated. Pick up a leaflet from the tourist office and ask for a
driver who can speak your language. Another alternative is to
take a minibus tour with an agency such as Blandy's.

The following tour is purely notional, picking out the
principal points of interest that any good tour (either by
minibus or taxi) will cover.

Heading around the island in an anti-clockwise direction,
the first stop is the lookout point of **Portela** (163 metres/535
feet). From here, you can survey the whole length of the gold-
en, sandy beach. Head north, however, and the desolate nature
of the landscape starts to become clear. Crop yield is poor,
partly because of the chronic lack of water, and fields which
were once tended are now deserted. Earning a living from
tourism here is often more appealing than toiling in the fields.

The island's highest peak, at 517 metres/695 feet, is Pico
do Facho, situated around 1.5 km (1 mile) due north of

*The island's last working windmill stands on a rotating
base so as to catch the wind from all directions.*

Portela, but you will need to don your walking boots if you wish to get to the summit. Its name, "peak of the torch," is taken from the warning beacons that were lit here in the days when French and Algerian pirates posed a threat to the island.

The circular road now arcs north to the minute village of **Camacha**, where the principal attraction is a picturesque old windmill. It is one of the last few still working on the island. If it is closed, ask one of the locals if you can look inside, and if it is convenient, they will fetch the friendly mill owner to come and open up for you (give him a tip for his trouble). Further local enterprise is in evidence near the mill, where a ramshackle winery with an antique wooden press produces the local Porto Santo wine. If it is closed, you can still sample the wine in either of the village's two restaurant-bars and, once again, speaking to some of the locals may secure you a brief look inside the winery—Camacha is a very small place.

A minor road heads west out of Camacha to **Fonte da Areia** ("the spring from the sandstone"), where the rugged coastline is particularly lovely. This is a pretty place, where the sandstone cliffs and rocks have weathered into interesting shapes and small, caves. A spring filtering through the rocks is the source of the island's mineral water. You can sample it fresh at the fountain by the café-bar.

The main road continues its loop, bringing you just about back to Vila Baleira, before a minor road heads north again towards **Pico do Castelo**. As the crow flies, it's only a couple of hundred yards from Pico do Facho, and from its height of 437 metres (1,433 feet) provides a quite commanding view itself. What's more, you can drive all the way here by car.

The old, rusted cannons are all that remain of the fortifications that once protected the islanders from pirates. Nowadays it's a popular spot for picnics and barbecues. (The grills are already here, just bring fuel and food.) Porto Santo's airfield lies just below. It is much larger than the one at Madeira (a fact of which the islanders are quite proud), and is used for both military and commercial aircraft, with new terminal facilities.

A favourite local picnic spot is **Morenos**, towards the southwest tip of the island, though close to, and looking out over, the north coast. It is neat and well-tended with sunshades, flowers, and seats, and enjoys a picturesque view over to the tiny Ilheu de Ferro (Isle of Iron). The last viewpoint of the tour is **Pico das Flores,** at 184 metres (603 feet). From here you can see north along the beach; the only blot on the landscape is the unfinished Novo Mondo hotel—a notorious, 8-storey white elephant that is completely out of proportion with the rest of the island.

Directly beneath Pico das Flores is the southern end of the beach and Porto Santo's easternmost point, known as **Ponta da Calheta**. The rest of the island's beach is a long, uninterrupted expanse, backed by attractive but slightly featureless dunes. Here, however, there are small bays with picturesque, rocky outcrops and you can enjoy a beautiful view across to the Ilheu de Baixo.

*With small bays and rock formations, Ponta de Calheta is Porto Santo's best beach.*

# WHAT TO DO

## SPORTS

With no beaches to speak of, and hardly enough flat ground for a playing surface, Madeira is not the first destination that springs to mind if you want a sporting holiday. Despite such limitations, however, there are still adequate opportunities for the active holidaymaker.

## Swimming

Although much of Madeira's coast runs steeply into the sea, offering little or no safe access for bathers, there are a number of stoney bays and beaches. Sadly, Madeira's one and only (black) sandy beach, at Prainha, is in an isolated location and is not very attractive. Better bets are Ponta do Sol and Ribeira Brava where, during summer, beach umbrellas are put up and locals and tourists crowd onto the pebbly shores. True beach lovers should hop islands, across to the sands of Porto Santo (though sunshine is only really guaranteed there from June to August).

Most of Madeira's good hotels have their own swimming pools, but if yours doesn't, year-round swimming is provided at the excellent Lido complex in Funchal's Tourist Zone. Here you will find two main pools, plus a children's pool, sunbathing along the terraces and rocks by the sea, and surprisingly good catering facilities. What's more, it is very cheap. The only drawback is, of course, the large crowds in summer. There is another good public pool where admission is also inexpensive in the Quinta Magnolia Park. Some of the larger hotels, such as the Savoy, also allow non-residents into their pool areas, but at a price that is guaranteed to exclude locals.

If you're touring the west of the island, don't forget to pack your swimming gear for the semi-natural lido at Porto Moniz. Ponta Delgada also has a public pool by the sea.

## Diving

The clear blue waters around Madeira have attracted the attention of four diving schools, for there is plenty worth seeing beneath the waves. Underwater reserves have been set up to protect the native marine life, and along with the abundant, multi-coloured fish, there are also many shipwrecks to explore.

Scorpio Divers, which is based at the old Lido (tel. 76 20 23), is the only British Sub-Aqua Club school; they offer everything from beginners' courses and single dives to advanced tuition. Alternative schools are the Atalaia Diving Club in Caniço (tel. 79 25 82), and the Urs Moser Diving School on Porto Santo (tel. 98 21 62), open from

*All aboard at Funchal marina for big-game fishing on well-fitted private charters.*

May to October; both of the above offer diving equipment hire and various courses.

## Big Game Fishing and Boat Trips

Once you're out of Madeira's shallow waters, you can—according to the season—catch blue marlin, bonito, tuna (big-eye, blue-fin, yellow-fin), barracuda, swordfish, wahoo, and shark (hammerhead, maco, and blue). The best deep-sea fishing is from June to September. The experts with whom you should get in touch are Turipesca (tel. 23 10 63), who set out from Funchal Marina.

Enquire at the Marina, also, about private boat charters. Tourist trips make regular departures from here.

## Windsurfing

Both the Lido and some of the larger hotels which face on to the ocean may rent out sailboards to non-clients, but there are no windsurfing schools on the island. Try Reid's and the Carlton in Funchal (the latter hires out pedaloes and canoes, too), the Dom Pedro Baia in Machico, and the hotels Roca-Mar and Galo-Mar in Caniço. **Waterskiing** is not so popular — you might try the Savoy.

During the summer months only, an itinerant windsurfing school offers tuition on neighbouring Porto Santo.

## Tennis

Flat land is at such a premium in Funchal that even the likes of Reid's and the Savoy have only two tennis courts each. If your hotel does not have its own court, try a neighbouring hotel, or perhaps an even better option is the Quinta Magnolia park, where the facilities are excellent (including floodlights) and very inexpensive. There are also squash courts and an exercise trail here.

## Walking

Thanks to a unique network of *levada* trails (see page 65), no island could be better placed to offer opportunities for walkers of all ages and abilities than Madeira. If, however, you want to get off the *levadas* and try either cross-country or mountain walking, the tourist office can supply you with details of the area from experienced guides.

*The courts of Quinta Magnolia park offer Madeira's best sporting bargain.*

## Horseback Riding

Tuition and cross-country riding are offered on Madeira by the Associação Hípica at Caminho dos Pretos, which is just outside Funchal. Horses can also be rented from the Riding Club of Choupana at Hotel Estrelicia (tel. 79 25 82).

## Golf

The 27-hole Campo de Golfe at Santo da Serra, which was opened in 1991, claims to be one of Europe's most exciting and spectacular golf courses, suitable for all levels. A club professional is on hand to offer tuition. The only drawback is the weather, for Santo da Serra has a wet micro-climate and fair-weather golf is relatively limited outside summer.

The recently opened Palheiro Golf Club, 15 minutes from the centre of Funchal, has an 18-hole course set in marvellous gardens with spectacular views back down to the town. It is an ideal place to visit, let alone to play golf.

## Spectator Sports

On Madeira, this means **football**. Funchal's premier team is in the first division of the Portuguese league, and you can enjoy good standards of play at the fine local stadium (on Rua Dr. Pita) during the season. See the local newspaper for current details.

# FESTIVALS

There are four major festivals a visitor to Madeira is bound to enjoy.

**Carnival**: Staged in February, Carnival is celebrated through the streets of Funchal with samba rhythms in the Brazilian style—but don't expect the hedonism or sensuality of the type of celebrations in Brazil or Spain. Funchal is much too restrained for that and, besides, this party is strictly small scale.

**Flower Festival**: This festival in April is a real favourite. Like the February Carnival, it includes floats—decorated in the most beautiful and inventive floral creations—parading through Funchal's streets.

There are two other events put on in addition to the main parade that should not be missed. One is the **children's parade**, in which each child carries a single flower, then places it in a hole in a specially made "wall" in the Praça do Município. This "Wall of Hope," as it is called, is a moving sight when complete. Once the parade is finished, an **exhibition** of the award-winning flowers and displays is put on in a lovely old house in Rua dos Castanheiros.

**Wine Festival**: In order to celebrate the September harvest, there are festivals in a number of villages. You may even see *boracheiros*, men carrying the traditional goat-skin bags once used to store and carry wine.

**New Year's Eve**: This is the biggest and most spectacular of the festivals, and one which has acquired a world-wide reputation. You will need to book accommodation many months in advance, and probably also pay a hefty premium. (Ironically, it's the one night of the year when you get the least sleep.) The itineraries of many winter cruise ships bring them into Funchal harbour on December 31, when their sirens compete with each other in a cacophony of sound. At 11:00 P.M., each house in Funchal switches on all its lights and opens all doors and windows, drenching the hillside in light. As the New Year rings in, a fantastic fireworks display begins (celebrations of one form or another have probably been going on since before Christmas).

Other events you may enjoy are: the thrilling **motor rally** in August, testing the skills of drivers from Madeira and all round the world on the island's tortuous roads; a **folk dancing festival** in Santana in July; and the **music festival**, which is held in June, and takes place mostly in Funchal's Teatro Municipal and Cathedral.

Several **religious festivals** also take place throughout the year, but one especially stands out. The **Feast of the Assumption**, known more parochially as the Festival of Nossa Senhora do Monte (Our Lady of Monte), is celebrated on 14 and 15 August in Monte. Pilgrims flock from all around the island to kiss the image of the patron saint, and some ascend the final 68 steps to the church on their knees.

The Madeirans see this pilgrimage as an obligation, since the Lady of Monte has brought them through troubled times. This spot is also something of a Lourdes to Madeirans, with sick and crippled visitors coming here in search of miracle cures. Once the pious devotions are over, however, wine flows, fireworks explode, *espetada* (kebab) stalls flourish, and Monte regains normality for another 363 days.

Other festivals to note are: 23-24 June, São João da Ribeira, Funchal; 28-30 June, São Pedro, Ribeira Brava; 9 September, Nosso Senhor dos Milagres, Machico.

Ask at the tourist office if there are any other festivals during the time of your visit.

## FOLKLORE

According to local by-laws, all Madeiran street flower-sellers have to wear native costume. You will thus see the ladies in cheerful colours alongside the cathedral, and also at the main city market.

Younger girls wear the same red-and-yellow striped skirts, often with a red bolero jacket and red cape, for folk-dance demonstrations. The men wear white linen trousers and white shirts, red cummerbunds, and occasionally, waistcoats. Curious black skull caps, with thin, curly tassels standing up like candlewicks, are worn by both men and women, and so are the native *botachãs* (literally, plain boots). These are made

### Dance Roots

The music and dances of Madeira go back to the earliest times and evoke rural and courtship rituals as well as less happy moments in the island's history. Dances imitating everyday work include jaunty jigs that illustrate crushing grapes with bare feet (a practice that has only recently died out) and carrying heavy baskets.

The happy rhythm of these dances contrasts with the downbeat *Dance of the Ponta do Sol*, which harks back to the days when Ponta do Sol was where the slaves lived. The steps are short, the feet hardly lift off the ground (because they were chained together), and the head is submissively bowed, since slaves were forbidden to look their masters in the eye.

from tanned ox hide and goat skin, and the uppers are often turned over. Women's boots are indicated by a red band.

Folk-dancing evenings are a regular feature at hotels, and one popular tour is a trip to Camacha's Café Relógio (see page 45), where the dancers are reputed to be Madeira's best.

Aside from the usual accordion, triangle, and drum, look out for the two musical instruments that are uniquely Madeiran. These are the *machête*, a guitar-like instrument that is plucked to a rather monotonous beat, and the extraordinary *brinquinho*, a percussion instrument that comes complete with tiny folk-dancing dolls holding bells and castanets. These are pressed together with an umbrella-like action, which causes them to slide up and down a central "maypole," thus clashing together the castanets and cymbals. At the same time, the *brinquinho* player twirls the instrument around.

*Madeirans uphold long traditions with frequent folklore dances and colourful native costumes.*

## ENTERTAINMENT

Although Madeira has a rather staid image when it comes to evening entertainment, there is enough nightlife in Funchal to keep most people happy.

The nucleus of the tourist nightlife scene is made up of the major hotels, and largely centres around the Casino Park Hotel (see page 129). Here you can play blackjack, French and American roulette, *chemin-de-fer*, and French Bank, and take a turn at the slot machines. An admission fee is charged and you will need to take your passport. If gambling isn't your scene, the Casino complex is also home to Baccara, the newest disco in town, where you can dance to the latest Euro-pop. Dinner shows are also staged here; theme nights are always well attended.

The other principal hotel for nightlife is the Carlton (see page 130), which puts on similar theme evenings, plus classical concerts and children's ballet shows. The Savoy (see page 130) also has a good reputation for offering lively nightlife.

Alternative types of entertainment available are sunset cruises (ask at the marina) and folklore evenings. For more down-to-earth nightlife, try in town, where a range of restaurants offer regular *fado* (literally meaning "fate") evenings. These include both Arsénios and Marcelinos in Funchal's old town, and O Pitéu on Rua da Carreira. *Fado* songs generally deal with the hardships of life. A woman singer dressed in black and accompanied by a pair of guitarists tries to wring a tear out of the audience, who listen in quiet respect. To see how the local youth pass their evenings, follow the crowd to Vespas Discoteca, which is on Avenida Sá Carneiro, or to any of the other venues around the capital.

Funchal's Teatro Municipal is the only place that regularly stages more highbrow entertainment. It is worth a visit, if only to see the theatre itself. Dating from 1888, it has recently been restored to its original splendour, and produces most of the performing arts. It is the centrepiece of the annual music festival which is held here in June.

## SHOPPING

Unlike its southern sisters, the Canary Islands, Madeira does not offer any tax concessions for visiting shoppers, so this is not the place to come in search of cheap electrical items, cameras, or watches. What is offered instead, however, is a long and proud craft heritage, and of course, some very fine natural products, such as flowers, wine, and liqueurs, which you can take back home to enjoy once your holiday is over.

### Where to Shop

Funchal's central area boasts the best variety of shops and local products on the island. There is little, if anything, that cannot be bought here, although it may be more fun, and quite possibly cheaper, to make your purchases closer to the source, in the villages. Moreover, the majority of Funchal's shops are small and personal—a reminder of the good old-fashioned days.

For the best possible introduction to all of the island's handicrafts and saleable products, visit the **Casa do Turista** on the seafront. Don't be put off by either the name or the initial impression—you may think you've stumbled into a small, stately home by mistake. After negotiating the first few rooms, which are carefully laid out with pieces of antique shelving displaying fragile breakables, it's quite a relief to find that the Casa do Turista is, after all, a fairly conventional department store. Don't miss the "mini-village" situated on the terrace at the back of the shop, where a little *palheiro* (see page 63), a house with a weaving loom and an old-fashioned shop re-create a small bit of old Madeira.

At the other end of the shopping scale, stalls selling handicrafts are set up at many of the major coach stops around the island (Cabo Girão and Eira do Serrado, for example), where you can often barter for hand-made items.

## What to Buy

**Needlework**: Embroidery and tapestry have long been two of Madeira's best known crafts, and in Funchal you will be able to visit factories or workshops where the final touches are put to these painstaking products. Table linens, sheets, dresses, blouses, and handkerchiefs are the sort of embroidery items for sale, while the tapestries range from copies of Old Master paintings to traditional scenes. There is, in fact, not much to see in terms of the items' manufacture, as the vast majority of the work is done in island homes by local women (estimates vary, but upwards of 10,000 are involved).

Funchal's factories do some needlework, ironing, packing, and, of course, act as showrooms. The biggest and best known one is Patrício & Gouveias, situated on Rua do Visconde de Anadia, where there are tours on weekdays, but

*Crafts of yesteryear—lace and needlework have both been popular in Madeira since 1850.*

keep an eye out for for other outlets marked by small signs in doorways. It's fun to explore these quaint places and there is rarely pressure to buy. Don't hope for bargains though; some of the table linen in particular is quite expensive, reflecting the effort that has gone into the end product.

To be sure that any needlework item is the genuine thing (as opposed to an inferior import), look for the IBTAM label. This stands for the *Instituto de Bordados, Tapeçarias e Artesanato da Madeira* (Institute of Madeiran Embroidery, Tapestry and Handicrafts) who also have a showroom on Rua Visconde de Anadia; their star work is a tapestry known as the Allegory of Madeira. This employed a total of 14 girls for three years and contains an estimated 7 million stitches.

**Wickerwork**: This important export trade for Madeira relies on locals working out of their own homes. The Café Relógio (see page 45) in Camacha is the best place to shop. It is an extraordinary world of wicker, with items ranging from the most conventional to the most implausible. Alternatively, there is also Sousa & Gonçalvez in Funchal's Rua do Castanheiro.

**Crafts**: If wicker or needlework doesn't appeal, then there are always the following:

*Boots*, made from soft goat hide, also part of the national costume. The seller just inside the entrance of Funchal market is worth a visit.

*Carved wooden models*, usually sailing boats.

*Marquetry*, a recently revived island craft, featured on small boxes and pictures, as well as on furniture.

*Pottery*, including pretty hand-painted plates, jugs, and jars.

*Straw hats*, old-style boaters, as worn by the *carreiros* who push the Monte toboggans.

*Knitwear*, cardigans, pullovers, or the distinctive bobble hats with earflaps which are still worn by workmen in the hills.

*Brinquinho*, Madeira's answer to the tambourine, in which miniature cymbals are clashed together by costumed dolls "dancing" round a maypole.

**Flowers**: Favourite souvenirs are orchids, flamingo flowers (*anthuriums*), and bird of paradise flowers (*strelitzias*); the latter in particular will last for a reasonable time once you are home. Most shops will box these for storage in the aircraft hold and deliver them either to your hotel or the airport on the day you leave. All the airlines are used to this procedure, and will label each package with a name tag to avoid confusion at the airport at the other end.

*Madeira's colourful and noisy brinquinho— an ingenious answer to the tambourine.*

Alternatively, if you have a spare pair of hands, you can carry them on the plane in bouquets, and if there is room they will be stowed carefully in the cabin.

**Food & Drink**: Madeira cake and wine are extremely long-lasting, so you can safely bring some back. Genuine Madeira cake, *bolo de mel* (or "honey cake"), is a far cry from what you get at home. This is a delicious, dark, heavy cake, similar to gingerbread and, despite its name, made from molasses, not honey. It lasts for a year.

Madeira wine is covered in detail under Eating Out (see page 94). Other drinks that you might want to take home include *branquinha* (*aguardente* with a stick of sugar-cane in the bottle), or a liqueur such as *licor de maracujá* (passion-fruit) or *ginja* (cherry liqueur).

# EATING OUT

There's no lack of restaurants in Funchal—the city has been catering for visitors since Victorian times. If you are after international or *haute* cuisine, the best places are the Hotel Zone, the up-market far end of the Old Town, or the touristy Marina establishments. If you would rather go native and eat with the locals, try the side streets around the cathedral, Rua Carreira, or the cheap part of the Old Town.

Restaurants known as *típicos* are basic eating places (often rustic, or decorated in a rustic style), where the menu is often limited to Madeiran specialities (*pratos típicos*). Prices are generally very reasonable. A trademark of a *típico* is the island bread, *bolo do caco*. This is unleavened and nearly always served with garlic butter (*com manteiga de alho*). Special *bolo do caco* stalls are set up at festivals.

A good *típico* is definitely worth a detour, but be aware that some of these have been spoiled by a constant stream of coach and cruise passengers and seem far more intent on extracting the tourist *escudo* than offering genuine Madeiran food. Away from the capital, the choice is often limited to just one or two local café-restaurants per village, though places on the tourist trail usually offer something smarter.

You will find a selection of recommended restaurants included at the end of this guide. If in doubt, remember the universal criterion for sizing up a local restaurant: are the locals eating there? (This does not apply, however, to some of the excellent gourmet restaurants to be found in Madeira's 5-star hotels.)

## Meal Times

Traditional opening times are kept to by most of Madeira's restaurants, with lunch (*o almoço*) served from around noon to 3:00 P.M. and dinner (*o jantar*) from around 7:00 to 10:00 P.M. Some restaurants in Funchal offer all day service and you will never have any problems finding cafés serving snacks, if not full meals.

When it comes to breakfast, Madeirans generally start their day with nothing more than a bread roll and a cup of coffee. Hotels, however, usually serve the standard international buffet, with bacon and eggs as well as cold meats, cheese, fruit and cereals.

## What to Eat

Madeira has typical dishes of its own rather than simply Portuguese specialities. As a rule, the food is simple, uses fresh ingredients, and is served up in hearty portions. Most establishments offer a Portuguese-International menu, which has Madeiran specialities, in addition to a free glass of Madeira wine when you first go in.

**Starters**: Soup is always on the menu. The best is usually Madeira's own *tomate e cebola*, a delicious soup made from tomatoes and onions, and very often served *com ovo* (with a poached egg floating on top). That Portuguese staple, *caldo verde*, is essentially a soup of cabbage, plus whatever else comes to hand (you can watch them shredding the cabbage in the market with a special machine). Another soup from the mainland is *açorda*, which is made with bread and garlic.

> *Casas de fados* or *adegas típicas* are restaurants where you can eat to the sound of the *fado*.

Basic fish restaurants serve *caramujos* (winkles), which look disgusting as you winkle them out from their tiny shells, but taste fine, and *lapas grelhadas* (grilled limpets). These are a meatier version of mussels (some of them taste almost like liver) and are served grilled in the shell.

At the other end of the price spectrum, look out for smoked swordfish (*espadarte fumado*), a Portuguese delicacy which is a little like smoked salmon, but tastes less sweet and has a coarser texture.

**Fish and Seafood**: the island's speciality is the *espada*, a fearsome-looking, jet black eel-like beast that can grow to around 1 metre (3 feet) in length, and has long, needle-sharp teeth. Don't worry though, you will never come across one while swimming, as they are fished from great depths. The most important thing for the diner is that their flaky, white flesh tastes delicious. Some restaurants will boil them, but more often they are fried, often with a banana, which complements the flavour surprisingly well.

The other island fish is tuna (*atum*), a solid, meaty-textured fish which is served in steaks (*bife de atum*) and often with a Madeira wine sauce (*a Madeirense*). Maize or cornmeal (*milho*) deep-fried in cubes (also an island speciality) is often served with tuna, and is offered as a standard accompaniment to many meals in *típicos* around the island.

You will also find a selection of other fish on the menu, usually grilled or fried, including: *pargo* and *besugo*,

*Drinking and dining al fresco are among the pleasures of Madeira at most times of the year.*

*Don't miss the fragrant herb and spice stalls on the top floor of Funchal market.*

which are types of sea-bream, plus *garoupa* and *cherne*, types of grouper. *Bacalhau* is the famous, Portuguese salt-cod, served in many ways. It is often served as a casserole, which tends to hide its distinctive, preserved flavour. Try it *cozido* (boiled). Other fish are shark, swordfish, and *bodião* (parrot-fish).

Two slow-simmering Portuguese favourites that appear on fish restaurant menus are *caldeirada* and (less frequently) *cataplana*. The former is a rich stew made from fish, potato, tomato, and onion, whereas the *cataplana* is actually the hinged pressure cooker, rather like a "double wok," into which goes a mixture of clams, ham, sausage, onion, garlic, parsley, white wine, and paprika. (Ingredients may vary according to what type of *cataplana* is on the menu.)

**Prato do dia (dish of the day) often offers you a good meal at a fair price.**

Two local favourites are octopus (*polvo*), served cold as a salad, hot, fried, or stewed; and squid (*lulas*), grilled, fried, or stuffed (*recheado*). Shellfish do not flourish in Madeiran waters, and all prawns and lobsters are imported.

**Meat**: *Espetada* (which is not to be confused with *espada*, see page 91) is the typical Madeiran meat dish, a kebab of beef which is traditionally threaded on a laurel stick. In most restaurants, however, it will be on a metal skewer with a hook on one end, which is hung vertically from a special stand, so just about everyone in the restaurant can see what you are eating. It's grilled over burning laurel, so its usually tasty, but it can also be rather tough. For something easier on the jaw, try pork in wine and garlic (*porco de vinho e alho*), which is marinaded, tenderized, and then grilled.

Chicken (*frango*) is always on the menu—whether it's served plain, grilled, African-style (as in *piri-piri*, when it's basted in a sauce of hot chilli peppers, then grilled), or in a Goan-inspired curry sauce.

Ox tongue (*língua*) served with Madeira wine sauce is another Portuguese speciality.

**Vegetables**: It would seem that "quantity rather than quality' is the ethos in most non-luxury restaurants. Boiled potatoes, rice, and tinned/frozen vegetables or salad are the standard accompaniments to the majority of meals. Occasionally, you will be offered sweet potato (*batata doce*), while yam (*inhame*) is a peculiar and very different type of accompaniment, served cold, sliced, and with molasses. You will only find this is in a *típico*.

**Desserts**: Portugal's *pudim* or *flan*, a type of *crème caramel*, is always available, as is ice-cream (*gelado*). After that, a good restaurant should be able to offer you seasonal fruit, but you may have to ask for it. The island has an excellent range, so sample it fresh from the market if not in a restaurant. A favourite is *anonas* or custard apple (from Peru). Split in half, the flesh is soft and white, with large black pips. To some its taste is like its name, a sort of custardy-apple, while others liken it (rather more fancifully) to strawberries and cream. A speciality of several tourist restaurants is fruit *flambé*.

## Table Wines

There is just the one brand of Madeiran table wine, *Atlantis Rosé*, and it is sold throughout the island. Aside from this, you may encounter the occasional local village wine, and most good restaurants stock a full range of Portuguese wines (top restaurants will also offer foreign labels).

> *á sua saude! -*
> **cheers (literally "to your health")**

*Vinho Verde* (literally "green wine") is named for its youth, rather than its colour, and has a slight fizz. It goes well with simple fish and seafood dishes.

Two quality Portuguese labels which are favourites at home and abroad are *Dão* and *Bairrada*—both come in red and white.

## Madeira Wine

The history of the island's eponymous drink, famous the world over, is as full and well-rounded as a bottle of the best vintage *Malvasia*.

When the island was first settled during the 15th century, Prince Henry ordered Zarco to plant vines, which were subsequently brought to the island from Crete. Al-

*There's never a shortage of fruits or vegetables at the lively Funchal market.*

though it was not intended that wine should become an important export trade, this is in fact what happened, thanks to a combination of its notable quality and the geographical position of Madeira on the shipping lanes to the East and West Indies. The island was an obvious stopping point where water, fresh food, and, of course, wine, could be taken on board. With the rise of the British colonies in North America and the West Indies, it was soon established as a favourite on both sides of the Atlantic, and shipped all over the British Empire.

Initially, Madeira was not a fortified wine, but gradually the addition of grape brandy became common practice in order to

## Fruits of the Season

Madeira has an excellent choice of exotic fruit all year round. The following list will tell you what to look for at the market, or what to ask for in a restaurant.

| | | |
|---|---|---|
| *January-June* | loquats | **nêsperas** |
| *January-March* | oranges | **laranjas** |
| *February-July* | strawberries | **morangos** |
| *May-June* | cherries | **cerejas** |
| *May-September* | papaya/paw-paw | **mamão** |
| *June-July* | plums | **ameixas** |
| | apricots | **alperces** |
| *June-October* | peach | **pêssego** |
| *July-September* | melon | **melão** |
| *July-October* | guava | **goiaba** |
| *August-October* | figs | **figos** |
| | passion fruit | **maracujá** |
| *August–December* | mango | **manga** |
| *September-October* | pomegranate | **romã** |
| *November-April* | custard apple | **anonas** |
| *December- February* | tangerines | **tangerinas** |
| *All year round* | bananas | **bananas** |

95

help to stabilize it on long sea voyages. During the 18th century, a chance discovery was made that shipping the wine actually improved its longevity as well as its flavour. After a while, producers realized that it was the heat of the Tropics which was responsible for this, and towards the end of the century, pipes of Madeira were loaded as ballast on transatlantic journeys in order to cook them as much as possible.

Later it became impractical to send barrels on round trips, and the conditions for heating the wine had to be reproduced at home. The easiest way was simply to store barrels in lofts which soaked up the abundant sunlight. Subsequent developments were special lodges called *estufas*, centrally heated by hot water pipes; this system is still in use today, subjecting each cask to a temperature of 35°C (95°F) for six months. It remains a mystery, though, how Madeira survives a process

## Madeira Wine — Lore and Legend

It was William Shakespeare who first gave Madeira wine a literary platform, when in *Henry IV* Falstaff is accused of selling his soul for a leg of chicken and a goblet of Madeira. (It seems of trifling importance that Henry IV actually died before the discovery of the island, let alone the wine!) In 1478, the Duke of Clarence went one better than Falstaff. Accorded the noble's privilege of electing his own means of execution, he chose to be drowned in a barrel of *Malmsey*.

The British have continued their love affair with the island wine down through the centuries. Sir Winston Churchill once ordered a bottle of 1792 vintage in Reid's Hotel, then further delighted his guests by placing a napkin over his arm and assuming the duties of waiter. Not to be left out, the Americans used it to toast the Declaration of Independence and the inauguration of George Washington (who allegedly drank a pint of Madeira daily at dinner). Benjamin Franklin and Thomas Jefferson were also Madeira connoisseurs.

which would ruin any other wine. Moreover, this process renders the wine virtually indestructible. A bottle of Madeira can be kept for many months uncorked without suffering any deterioration, even when other types of fortified wine would deteriorate quickly under such conditions.

**Choosing a Bottle**. There are four types of Madeira, each named after the grape which gives that style of wine its distinctive flavour and characteristics. The driest is *Sercial*, which has a full-bodied, nutty flavour, not unlike an *amontillado* sherry. This is best served chilled as an aperitif. *Verdelho*, which is classified as medium-dry, should be served slightly chilled. As well as being an aperitif, it's also recommended as an accompaniment to soup. *Bual*, a rich and port-like Madeira with a splendid honeyed taste, has an underlying acidity, which means that it can cut through sweet desserts and is also a good accompaniment to cheese. Finally and most famously, *Malvasia* (also known as *Malmsey*) is the richest of all, and is usually served following a meal.

All the Madeira wines, with the exception of vintage, are made from blends of several years, the youngest component

*Madeira's wonderfully blended wines have satisfied Shakespeare and other historical figures.*

of the blend being the stated age of the wine on the label; *Finest* is a blend in which the youngest is at least three years old, and *Reserve* and *Special Reserve* wines are at least five and ten years old, respectively. The very best, however, are *Vintage* wines, produced with the crop of a single type of grape from a single year, and only bottled after ageing in oak casks for a minimum of 20 years. It is a general rule that the longer the wine stays in the cask, the better it will be. The wine is then kept for another two years before sale.

If you really want to impress the folks back home, buy a bottle of *Blandy's 1863 Vintage Bual* from the São Francisco Wine Lodge—it's a mere 51,000 escudos. If your budget doesn't stretch to that, you can pick up a more recent vintage for around 6,000 escudos.

## Tea or Coffee?

Asking for a tea or coffee in Madeira is not as easy as you might think. Tea is *chá*, though you will also have to ask for milk (*com leite*) or lemon (*com limão*) unless you want it black. If you ask for *chá* in a locals' café, however, you may well be served a cup of boiling water with a slice of lemon in it. This is known as *chá de limão*.

Coffee is *café*, but if a Madeiran wants a small, black, strong coffee, he will ask for a *bica*. If more is required he will order a *duplo* (double), which is a large *bica*. Add a little hot water to a *bica* and it becomes a *carioca*.

A small coffee with a dash of milk is known as a *garoto*. A large white coffee is a *Chinesa*, and if you like your coffee very milky, then ask for a *galão*, which comes in a long glass. If you prefer it decaffeinated, ask for a *sem cafeína*, and you will be given a small sachet of instant decaffeinated coffee.

## Other Island Drinks

The most famous island drink after Madeira is *aguardente*, a powerful sugarcane distillation, which varies in taste from virtually unpalatable firewater to smooth, aged brandy. Look for the term *velha* (old) on the label unless you have an iron constitution.

Add lemon juice and honey to *aguardente* and you have *poncha*, a delicious drink that belies its ferocious base. The hard-drinking men of Câmara de Lobos fortify themselves with it before and after fishing trips, and you will find *poncha* all over Madeira (though lacking the potency of that at Câmara de Lobos).

Other liqueurs are distilled from the island's fruit, two notable examples being a cherry brandy from Curral das Freiras (see page 44) called *ginja*, and *licor de maracujá*, passion-fruit liqueur (don't confuse it with the soft drink, *maracujá*). The local lager, *Coral*, is also an excellent beverage. If you don't drink, you may enjoy the bottled mineral water that is produced in Porto Santo, but this can be an acquired taste.

### *To Help You Order...*

| Could we have a table? | | **Queríamos uma mesa** | |
|---|---|---|---|
| I'd like a/an/some... | | **Queria...** | |
| bread | **pão** | pepper | **pimenta** |
| butter | **manteiga** | potatoes | **batatas** |
| coffee | **um café** | rice | **arroz** |
| dessert | **uma sobremesa** | salad | **uma salada** |
| fish | **peixe** | salt | **sal** |
| fruit | **fruta** | sandwich | **sanduiche** |
| ice-cream | **um gelado** | soup | **uma sopa** |
| meat | **carne** | sugar | **açucar** |
| menu | **a ementa** | tea | **chá** |
| milk | **leite** | wine | **vinho** |

| | | | |
|---|---|---|---|
| **alho** | garlic | **frito** | fried |
| **amêijoas** | baby clams | **gambas** | prawns |
| **ananás** | pineapple | **gelado** | ice-cream |
| **arroz** | rice | **grão-de-bico** | chick-pea |
| **assado** | roast | **guisado** | stew |
| **atum** | tunny/tuna | **laranja** | orange |
| **azeitonas** | olives | **legumes** | vegetables |
| **bacalhau** | cod (salted) | **leitão** | suckling pig |
| **banana** | banana | **linguado** | sole |
| **besugo** | sea-bream | **lombo** | fillet |
| **bife (vaca)** | steak (beef) | **lulas** | squid |
| **bolo** | cake | **maçã** | apple |
| **borrego** | lamb\ | **mariscos** | shellfish |
| **bremesa** | dessert | **melancia** | watermelon |
| **cabrito** | kid | **mexilhões** | mussels |
| **camarões** | shrimp | **molho** | sauce |
| **caranguejo** | crab | **morangos** | strawberries |
| **cavala** | mackerel | **ovo** | egg |
| **cebola** | onion | **pargo** | bream |
| **chouriço** | spicy sausage | **peixe** | fish |
| **churrasco** | grilled meat | **perú** | turkey |
| **coelho** | rabbit | **pescada** | hake |
| **cogumelos** | mushrooms | **pescadinha** | whiting |
| **costeletas** | chops | **pêssego** | peach |
| **cozido** | boiled | **porco** | pork |
| **dobrada** | tripe | **presunto** | ham |
| **enguias** | eel | **queijo** | cheese |
| **ervilhas** | peas | **robalo** | bass |
| **estufado** | stewed/braised | **salmonete** | red mullet |
| **feijões** | beans | **salsichão** | large sausage |
| **figos** | figs | **sotorrada** | toast |
| **framboesas** | raspberries | **uvas** | grapes |
| **frango** | chicken | **vitela** | veal |

# INDEX

# HANDY TRAVEL TIPS

An A–Z Summary of Practical Information

**A**

**ACCOMMODATION** (See also CAMPING on page 105 and the selection of RECOMMENDED HOTELS starting on page 129)

Hotels and hotel-apartments in Madeira are graded from 2 stars to 5 stars. Below the rating of hotel is *estalagem*, which loosely translates as "inn," though these are to all intents simply a hotel away from the main tourist area. Below *estalagem* are *albergaria*, *residência*, and *pensão*. These are usually bed and breakfast hotels with only basic facilities. The quality of *residências* and *pensões* is variable, so don't accept a room without inspecting it. If you only want comfortable, simple accommodation, without television, sea view etc, then these are much cheaper and often provide more personal service.

Madeira is unique in also offering *quinta* accommodation. *Quintas* are gracious mansions, usually set in splendid gardens, brimming with antiques, and restored to offer a standard of accommodation equivalent to a 4- or 5-star hotel. Due to their size and the nature of the building, they cannot offer all the sporting or social facilities of a top hotel, but in terms of character and personal service they are often much better. *Quintas* are consequently often as expensive as 4- and 5-star hotels, despite a *residência* or lower rating. All are limited in number of rooms, so book early. Early booking is also recommended if you want to stay on the island on New Year's Eve (see page 81).

State-run *pousadas* offer the chance to experience local hospitality and cuisine. There are two *pousadas* on Madeira: the Pousada dos Vinháticos on the north-south road from Ribeira Brava to São Vicente, and the Pousada do Pico do Arieiro, on top of the mountain of the same name. In keeping with the general *pousada* principal, these both enjoy tranquil, scenic settings away from the main tourist areas.

| | |
|---|---|
| I'd like a single/double room. | **Queria um quarto simples/duplo.** |
| with bath/shower | **com banho/chuveiro** |
| What's the rate per night? | **Qual é o preço por noite?** |

## AIRPORT *(aeroporto)*

Madeira's Santa Catarina airport at Santa Cruz has one of the shortest passenger runways in Europe. Indeed, in order to ensure take-off, some flights have to reduce weight by carrying only partly-full fuel tanks. They then make the short (15-minute) flight to Porto Santo, fill the tanks, and take off again from the regular-sized runway there. Santa Catarina runway is being extended (completion in 1999); meanwhile, nervous passengers are advised not to look out the window on take-off, as the runway literally drops straight into the sea. Don't let this put you off, however, for Madeira airport has an excellent safety record. If you are travelling to Porto Santo, you will still fly into Madeira, then fly or sail from there.

The airport lies 22 km (14 miles) east of Funchal. It's a good, straight road and as long as you avoid rush hour, only takes 30 minutes by taxi or about an hour by bus. Trolleys are available for arriving passengers, but there are no baggage porters. There is a choice of several car hire firms with service desks at the airport, while elsewhere in the terminal is a small tourist information stand, currency-exchange office, restaurant and bar, souvenir shop, and a very limited-range duty-free shop. The airport on Porto Santo is used as a local stop by a subsidiary of TAP Air Portugal, and there are some direct flights from Lisbon and Orporto.

Where can I get a taxi?     **Onde posso encontrar um táxi?**

## CAMPING *(campismo)*

Madeira has two official campsites, at Porto Moniz on the northwest tip of the island, and at Ponta do Sol on the south coast (currently suffering disruption due to major road building — check to see whether the situation has improved nearer the time of your visit). For further details write to: Club de Campismo da Madeira, Rua Queimada de Baixo, 32, 9000 Funchal; tel. (091) 22 89 16.

## Madeira

The tourist information office also recommends sites at both Chão dos Louros, close to Encumeada on the São Vicente-Ribeira Brava road, and near Ribeira de Santa Luzia, set off the road from Monte to Poiso. Both of these are rather isolated, but do have some facilities. Porto Santo has one official site, set in a good location next to the beach, just a few hundred yards from Vila Baleira. For more details write to: Parque de Campismo do Porto Santo, Vila Baleira, 9400 Porto Santo, Madeira; tel. (091) 98 21 60.

| Is there a campsite near here? | **Há algum parque de campismo por aqui perto?** |
| May we camp here? | **Podemos acampar aqui?** |
| We have a caravan (trailer). | **Temos uma roulotte.** |

**CAR HIRE** *(carros de aluguer)* (See also DRIVING on page 109 and PLANNING YOUR BUDGET on page 117)

Local car hire firms compete with major international organizations in Funchal and at the airport. Prices vary significantly, so shop around. You must be at least 21 (23 for some firms) and have held a valid national (or international) driving licence for at least one year. You will need to present a recognized credit card (or a large cash deposit) when booking. Third-party insurance is always included in the basic charge, but many firms quote collision damage waiver (CDW) as an extra. Without this you could be liable for any damage or loss to your vehicle, however caused, so you are strongly advised to take it. Since your general travel insurance policy will normally cover you in the event of personal accident or loss of baggage, you should not need personal accident insurance (PAI) or any form of theft coverage, but double-check your own policy to be on the safe side. Some companies include CDW, theft of vehicle protection, baggage protection and PAI in a total package which cannot be split. On top of all this, a government tax of 12% is added to the total rental bill when booking locally.

| I'd like to hire a car. | **Queria alugar um carro.** |
|---|---|
| tomorrow | **para amanhã** |
| for one day/week | **por um dia/uma semana** |

## CHILDREN IN MADEIRA

Apart from top-of-the-range places, there's never a problem taking children into restaurants or bars. There is, however, little for older children to do on the island. The beach at Porto Santo, the lido at Funchal, and the stuffed animals at the Museu Municipal are the main attractions for them. They may also enjoy the Monte toboggan, though by "thrill ride" standards it is pretty tame.

## CLIMATE

Madeira is generally warm all year and is a famous winter retreat for north Europeans. Beware, though; the winter months are relatively wet and the winds get noticeably stronger. The rainiest period is from October to December, with an average of 6 to 7 days of rain per month, but you can still usually count on an average of 6 hours of sunshine a day. From May to September the air is warm and a little humid. The typical pattern, all year round, is a clear, bright morning, with clouds rolling down from the mountains in the afternoon. Funchal generally has the best weather on the island. If you want warm, clear weather for mountain walking, go in summer.

| | | J | F | M | A | M | J | J | A | S | O | N | D |
|---|---|---|---|---|---|---|---|---|---|---|---|---|---|
| Average daily | °C | 13 | 13 | 13 | 14 | 16 | 17 | 19 | 19 | 19 | 18 | 16 | 14 |
| minimum | °F | 56 | 56 | 56 | 58 | 60 | 63 | 66 | 67 | 67 | 65 | 61 | 58 |
| Average daily | °C | 19 | 18 | 19 | 19 | 21 | 22 | 24 | 24 | 24 | 23 | 22 | 19 |
| maximum | °F | 66 | 65 | 66 | 67 | 69 | 72 | 75 | 76 | 76 | 74 | 71 | 67 |
| Sea | °C | 17 | 17 | 17 | 17 | 18 | 19 | 20 | 21 | 22 | 23 | 20 | 18 |
| temperature | °F | 63 | 63 | 63 | 63 | 64 | 66 | 68 | 70 | 72 | 73 | 68 | 64 |

## CLOTHING

Sunny-weather clothes will be fine in summer, but pack a pullover for mountain excursions. Winters are mild with the occasional shower, so a light, rainproof jacket may come in handy. Also in winter, you will definitely need woollies (and waterproofs) for inland trips. If you're planning on walking you will need sensible footwear, but unless you are intent on tackling some of the more arduous trails, you won't need walking boots.

Although there's less formality on Madeira these days, after 7pm in Reid's restaurants and bars men must wear a dark suit and tie. If you are patronizing a luxury hotel or restaurant in Funchal, jacket and tie are generally expected so you won't feel overdressed in a suit. In nightspots such as the casino, a certain degree of "dressing up" never goes amiss.

## COMPLAINTS

As a first principle, always try to sort out any difficulties immediately with the manager or proprietor of the establishment concerned. If you are unable to resolve your problem, inform the local tourist office and, in serious cases, ask them to enlist the assistance of the local police (though on Madeira this would be an extremely rare occurrence).

## CRIME

Although Madeira really is one of the safest places in the world for tourists, factors such as poverty (which does exist here) inevitably make temptation irresistible for some. Follow the same general rules that you would elsewhere. Never leave anything of value in your car, even if it is out of sight. Burglaries of holiday apartments are rare, but leave any valuables in a safe-deposit box, or with the hotel reception. You must report any losses to the local police within 24 hours and obtain a copy of your statement for insurance purposes.

## CUSTOMS and ENTRY FORMALITIES (alfândega)

Most visitors, including citizens of all EU countries, the USA, Canada, Eire, Australia and New Zealand, need only a valid passport — no visa — to enter Madeira.

The following chart shows the main duty-free items that visitors (18 and over) may carry into Madeira, and into your own country:

| Into: | Cigarettes | | Cigars | | Tobacco | Spirits | | Wine | |
|---|---|---|---|---|---|---|---|---|---|
| Portugal | 200 | or | 50 | or | 250 g | 1 $l$ | or | 2 $l$ | |
| Australia | 200 | or | 250 | or | 250 g | 1 $l$ | or | 1 | $l$ |
| Canada | 200 | and | 50 | and | 900 g | 1.1 $l$ | or | 1.1 | $l$ |
| N. Zealand | 200 | or | 50 | or | 250 g | 1.1 $l$ | and | 4.5 | $l$ |
| S. Africa | 400 | and | 50 | and | 250 g | 1 $l$ | and | 2 | $l$ |
| U.S.A. | 200 | and | 100 | and | *) | 1 $l$ | or | 1 $l$ | |

*) A reasonable quantity.

**Currency restrictions**. Tourists may bring an unlimited amount of Portuguese or foreign currency into Madeira. No more than 100,000 escudos or the equivalent of 500,000 in foreign currency may be exported per person per trip.

I've nothing to declare.          **Não tenho nada a declarar.**
It's for my personal use.         **É para uso pessoal.**

**DRIVING**

There are many good reasons not to drive on Madeira; car-hire and petrol are expensive, taxis are relatively cheap, the tortuous interior roads can be hard work, and so on. But if there are many cons, then some of the pros may be equally compelling. You may well enjoy the challenge of those tortuous roads, and, of course, you have maximum flexibility with your own set of wheels.

**Driving conditions**. The rules are the same as on the Continent: drive on the right, overtake on the left, yield right of way to all vehicles coming from your right. Speed limits are nominally 90 k/mh (56 mph) outside built-up areas and 60 k/mh (37 mph) in built-up areas. Average cross-country speeds are well below 60 k/mh. It is only worth considering driving into Funchal if you are staying well outside town (at Machico or Garajau, for instance). If you do, expect traffic jams.

**Parking**. Funchal is well served by reasonably priced car parks at either end of town. Parking in the centre is virtually impossible. You will have few difficulties elsewhere on the island.

**Rules and regulations**. Seatbelts must be worn and children under 12 are not allowed in the front seats. Motorcycle helmets should also be worn at all times.

**Breakdowns**. If you belong to a motoring organization affiliated with the Automóvel Clube de Portugal (ACP), you can make use of their services free of charge. The Funchal office is at Rua Dr. António José Almeida 17-2°; tel. (091) 22 36 59. You will have no problem finding well-equipped garages in Funchal, but elsewhere you may have to rely on the services of the local mechanic.

**Road signs**. Aside from the standard international pictographs, you may encounter the following:

| | |
|---|---|
| **Alto** | Halt |
| **Cruzamento** | Crossroads |
| **Curva perigosa** | Dangerous bend (curve) |
| **Descida íngreme** | Steep hill |
| **Desvio** | Diversion (Detour) |
| **Encruzilhada** | Crossing |
| **Estacionamento permitido/ proibido** | Parking permitted/ No parking |
| **Guiar com cuidado** | Drive with care |
| **Máquinas em manobras** | Road works (men working) |
| **Obras** | Road works (men working) |
| **Paragem (de autocarro)** | Bus stop |
| **Pare** | Stop |
| **Pedestres, peões** | Pedestrians |
| **Perigo** | Danger |

| | |
|---|---|
| **Proibida a entrada** | No entry |
| **Seguir pela direita/esquerda** | Keep right/left |
| **Sem saída** | No through road |
| **Trabalhos** | Road works (men working) |

| | |
|---|---|
| Are we on the right road for...? | **É esta estrada para...?** |
| Fill the tank, please with... | **Encha o depósito de...** |
| three star/four star | **normal/super** |
| I've broken down. | **O meu carro está avariado.** |
| There's been an accident. | **Houve um acidente.** |

**Fluid measures**

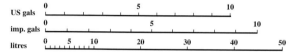

**Distance**

**E**

## ELECTRIC CURRENT *(corrente eléctrica)*

The standard current is 220-volt, 50 cycle AC. Transformers and plug adaptors are required for American appliances.

## EMBASSIES and CONSULATES *(embaixada; consulado)*

Several countries maintain consuls in Funchal. For serious matters, people are usually referred to their embassy in Lisbon.

**American Consular Agency**: Avenida Luís de Camões, Ed. Infante, Block B, 4th floor; tel. (091) 74 34 29

**British Consular Agency** (also for Commonwealth citizens): Avenida Zarco, 2; tel. (091) 22 12 21

# Madeira

## Lisbon Embassies

**Australia**: 4th Floor, Avenida da Liberdade, 244; tel. (01) 52 33 50

**Canada**: Avenida da Liberdade, 144; tel. (01) 347 48 92

**Eire**: 4th Floor, Rua da Imprensa e Estrela, 1; tel. (01) 396 15 69

**South Africa**: Avenida Luís Bivar 10/10A; tel. (01) 53 50 41

**UK**: Rua São Domingos à Lapa, 37; tel. (01) 396 11 91

**USA**: Avenida Forças Armadas, 16; tel. (01) 726 66 00

Most embassies and consulates are open Monday to Friday, from 9 or 10am until 5 or 6pm, with a lunch break lasting 1–2 hours.

**EMERGENCIES** *(urgência)* (See also MEDICAL CARE page 116)

The emergency number anywhere in Madeira for police, fire or ambulance is **115**.

| **Fire** | 22 21 22 | (Funchal) |
|---|---|---|
| | 96 51 83 | (Machico) |
| | 52 41 63 | (Santa Cruz) |

The new Funchal hospital has a 24-hour emergency ward. Outside Funchal, ask for the local *Centro de Saúde* (Health Centre). These are usually well-signposted but may have limited opening hours.

## ETIQUETTE

The people of Madeira, like the Portuguese in general, are less outgoing than many Europeans, but they are usually very friendly, without pretensions, and it's not too difficult to strike up a conversation. Don't let it bother you if some villagers seem to be staring at you; it's only unaffected curiosity. However, it's often difficult to catch the eye of a waiter when you want one. The Portuguese have no equivalent for "Waiter!" but the term *Faz favor!* ("Please!") will suffice.

| How do you do/Pleased to meet you. | **Muito prazer.** |
|---|---|
| How are you? | **Como está?** |

Very well, thank you.        **Muito bem, obrigado/obrigada (masc/fem speaker).**

# G

**GETTING TO MADEIRA** (See also AIRPORT on page 105)

There are regular cheap charter flights to Madeira from Britain and most major cities in western Europe. The only airline flying scheduled services directly to Funchal is GB Airways; all other scheduled services fly via Lisbon.

The flight time from London to Madeira is around 3 hours 30 minutes, and from Lisbon to Madeira 1 hour 30 minutes. Until recently it was possible to sail to Madeira by cargo ship, but they no longer take passengers. Big cruise liners stop off at the island, but often only long enough for a brief sightseeing tour.

**GUIDES and TOURS** (See also TAXIS on page 124)

The favourite way of seeing Madeira is by coach. There are several operators who basically all go to the same places, but charge different rates for different services. At the top end of the market are companies such as Blandy's, who employ very knowledgable guides. (Blandy's is the only company who runs single language tours, thus sparing you the chore of listening to the same commentary in other translations.) Other companies cut prices by using taped commentaries. Standard itineraries include: West of the Island; East of the Island, including Pico do Arieiro; a half-day covering Monte/Curral das Freiras/Picos dos Barcelos; guided *levada* walks; and jeep safaris to out-of-the-way places such as Boca dos Namorados (see page 44) or the wilder parts of Paúl da Serra. Not all of these are good value; the *levada* walk and the Monte trip are quite easy, and much cheaper to do by yourself.

Other tour operator itineraries cover a day-trip to Porto Santo, including an island tour (this is only recommended in summer, when sunshine and calm sailing are the norm), but you can also make your own way to the island and take a half-day minibus tour. Half-day boat trips cruise up and down the Madeiran coast, while other outings from Funchal Marina include a trip to the Ilhas Desertas, or a full day's sailing, including lunch, free wine, and the opportunity for swimming. If you would like a personal guide to a particular place, enquire at the tourist office in Funchal, where they keep the names of specialized *levada* and walking guides. Alternatively, go to the guides association, which is situated at Rua Dr. Brito da Câmara, 4, Apt 103; tel. (091) 22 65 24.

| | |
|---|---|
| We'd like an English-speaking guide/an English interpreter. | **Queremos um guia que fale inglês/um intérprete de inglês.** |

# L

## LANGUAGE

(For further useful expressions see the cover of this guide)

The language of Madeira is Portuguese. Your high school Spanish will help you read signs and menus, but the spoken language is much more difficult to master. In Funchal and most villages on the tourist trail, most Madeirans understand and speak at least a little English. The Berlitz PORTUGUESE PHRASEBOOK AND DICTIONARY covers most situations that you're likely to encounter. Also useful is the Berlitz Portuguese-English/English-Portuguese pocket dictionary, which contains a special menu-reader supplement.

## USEFUL EXPRESSIONS

| | |
|---|---|
| goodbye | **adeus** |
| goodnight | **boa noite** |
| excuse me/you're welcome | **perdão/da nada** |
| where/when/how | **onde/quando/como** |
| how long/how far? | **quanto tempo/a que distância?** |
| yesterday/today/tomorrow | **ontem/hoje/amanhã** |
| day/week/month/year | **dia/semana/mês/ano** |
| left/right | **esquerdo/direito** |
| cheap/expensive | **barato/caro** |

| | |
|---|---|
| hot/cold | **quente/frio** |
| old/new | **velho/novo** |
| open/closed | **aberto/fechado** |
| free (vacant)/occupied | **livre/ocupado** |
| early/late | **cedo/tarde** |
| What does this mean? | **Que quer dizer isto?** |
| Please write it down. | **Escreva-mo, por favor.** |
| Have you something less expensive? | **Tem qualquer coisa de mais barato?** |
| Help me, please. | **Ajude-me, por favor.** |
| Get a doctor, quickly. | **Chame um médico, depressa.** |

**LOST PROPERTY** *(objectos perdidos)*

If you lose something, go to the police station on Rua João de Deus in Funchal, which operates a lost property office. If your item is not here, at least report the loss and they will issue an official form for you to complete for your own insurance purposes. Outside Funchal, try the local police station.

| | |
|---|---|
| I've lost my... | **Perdi... a minha carteira/o meu** |
| wallet/bag/passport | **saco/o meu passaporte** |

## MAPS

Madeira is a small island with relatively few roads, so orientation is easy. Detailed maps are published by the Instituto Geográfico e Cadastral, obtainable at local bookshops. The best map available in Britain is the Bartholomew Holiday Map. Walkers should buy a copy of *Landscapes of Madeira* by John and Pat Underwood (published by Sunflower Books), which includes specially drawn walking tour maps and details many *levada* trails. The tourist information offices in Funchal and Porto Santo will supply you with a free map which includes both the island and capital.

## MEDICAL CARE
(See also Emergencies on page 112)

Funchal has a good new hospital, Cruz de Carvalho (tel. (091) 74 21 11), with doctors who speak English and other foreign languages. For minor ailments, call in at a Health Centre (*Centro de Saúde*). There are several of these around the island and in Funchal. Tourist offices carry lists of doctors and dentists who speak English. Travel insurance to cover medical expenses is always sensible, and EU residents should also obtain form E111 before departure. This entitles you to free medical treatment while on holiday in Madeira. If you don't take the form with you, it's a matter of paying there and claiming back on your travel insurance later.

Common ailments include sunburn, through too much exposure too soon (take it easy to begin with and never fall asleep in the sun), and hangovers from an excess of alcohol (not helped by the devil-may-care spirit measures). Mosquitoes are present in summer, so an anti-mosquito device which simply plugs into your wall and emits a vapour that is noxious to the insect, but not to you, is worthwhile (available at airport shops). Chemists (*farmácias*) have a green cross sign and are open during normal shop hours (see Opening Hours on page 120). After hours, each pharmacy takes it in turns to open late; its name and location will be posted in the windows of the others.

| | |
|---|---|
| Where's the nearest (all night) pharmacy? | **Onde fica a farmácia (de serviço) mais próxima?** |
| I need a doctor/dentist. | **Preciso de um médico/dentista.** |
| an ambulance/hospital | **uma ambulância/hospital** |
| sunburn/a fever | **queimadura de sol/febre** |
| an upset stomach | **dôr de estômago** |

## MONEY MATTERS
(See also Customs and Entry Formalities on page 108)

**Currency**. Price tags carry the $ sign, but here it means *escudo* (abbreviated to esc) and the sign often replaces the decimal point, so

50$00 means 50 escudos. Coins in use are 1, 2, 5, 20, 50, 100, and 200 escudos. Bank notes come in denominations of 500, 1,000 (known as one conto), 2,000, 5,000, and 10,000 escudos.

**Banking hours** are generally from 8:30am to 3pm Monday to Friday. Beware that changing money can be outrageously expensive — all banks either levy up to 12% in commission or charge a flat fee of around £10/$20 (dollars), regardless of amount changed, so ask first. It may be best to use either your hotel or a *bureau de change*, and shop around for the lowest rate of commission. Automatic money-exchanging machines can also be found in Funchal.

**Credit cards, traveller's cheques, Eurocheques**. Although these are accepted in most establishments, paying by cheque is invariably more expensive than by cash, due to the lower rate of exchange.

| | |
|---|---|
| Can I pay with this credit card? | **Posso pagar com este este cartão de credito?** |
| Where's the nearest bank/ currency exchange office? | **Onde fica o banco mais próximo/ a casa de câmbio mais próxima?** |
| I want to change some pounds/dollars. | **Queria trocar dólares.** |
| Can I cash a traveller's cheque? | **Posso trocar um cheque de viagem?** |
| How much is that? | **Quanto custa isto?** |

PLANNING YOUR BUDGET

The following list will give you some idea of what to expect in Madeira. It's impossible to keep up with inflation, so please consider these as approximations and add a small contingency figure on top.

**Airport Transfer**. Bus to centre of Funchal 500 esc, taxi 5,000 esc, add around 500 esc to reach the Tourist Zone (fare supplement of 20% at weekends, public holidays, and between 10pm and 7am).

**Babysitters**. 2,000 esc per hour (more after midnight).

**Big-game fishing**. 25,000 esc per person per day, spectators 5,000 esc.

## Madeira

**Camping**. 450 esc per person, 300-800 esc per tent per night.

**Car hire**. Price for one day, local companies (international companies' prices follow) inclusive of CDW and 12% government tax.

*Group 0/A*: Fiat Panda/Seat Marbella: 4,500–5,800 esc (6,300––6,800 esc).

*Group A/B*: Renault Clio/Ford Fiesta 3-door: 4,000–5,500 esc (5,600 esc).

*Group B/C*: Renault Clio/Ford Fiesta 5-door: 6,000–7,000 esc (6,500 esc).

**Entertainment**. Casino (admission only) 800 esc, casino plus show and dinner 8,000 esc. Folklore night (including dinner and show) 5,000–8,000 esc.

**Excursions**. Madeira coach trips: all prices from Funchal (add 300-500 esc for other pick-up points).

*Full day trips (including lunch) with guide commentary*: East Madeira 7,000 esc; West Madeira 7,000 esc; Jeep safari 8,000 esc.

*Half-day trips with guide commentary*: *levada* walk 4,000 esc; Monte, Curral das Freiras and Pico dos Barcelos 5,000 esc (4,000 esc).

*Boat trips*: Half-day 5,000 esc; full day with lunch 8,000 esc. Twilight cruise 4,000 esc; Funchal-Porto Santo, including island tour, 16,000 esc.

*Porto Santo*: Island tour by minibus 2,000 esc per person; island tour by taxi 4,000 esc per cab.

**Gardens**. Jardim Botânico 300 esc; Boa Vista Orchid Farm 300 esc; Palheiro Gardens 800 esc; Monte Palace Tropical Gardens 1,000 esc.

**Hotels**. (Double room with bath/shower per night) 3-star hotel 9,000–15,000 esc; 4-star hotel 12,000–22,000 esc; 5-star hotel 30,000–38,000 esc; 3- or 4-star *residência* 5,000–8,000 esc; *pousadas* 11,000–13,000 esc.

**Island-hopping**. Madeira-Porto Santo connections: by air 13,600 esc return, 6,800 esc one way; by boat 8,700 esc same day return, 6,600 esc ordinary return, 4,000 esc one way.

**Meals and drinks**. Three course meal per person excluding drinks, in a reasonable establishment 2,200–3,500 esc; tea/coffee 60–120 esc; beer 100–150 esc; soft drink 80-100 esc.

**Motorcycle hire**. Porto Santo only, 7,500 esc per day (including CDW and 12% government tax).

**Museums**. 200–450 esc (some free).

**Petrol**. Per litre: Super 156 esc, unleaded 158 esc.

**Shopping bag**. Small loaf of bread 100 esc, butter (250g) 160 esc, milk (1 litre) 134 esc, tomatoes 260 esc per kg, chicken 370 esc per kg, pork chops/escalope of veal 950 esc per kg, instant coffee (50g) 360 esc, ground coffee (250g) 415 esc, orange juice (1 litre) 225 esc, bottle of table wine from 350 esc, bottle Madeira wine from 700 esc.

**Sports**. Tuition for most sports 5,000-6,000 esc per hour.

*Diving*: Single dive 5,000 esc, novice diver course (including equipment hire) 49,500 esc.

*Golf*: Green fees – 9 holes 4,500 esc, 18-holes 7,000 esc. Club and trolley hire – 9 holes 2,350 esc, 18 holes 3,350 esc. Tuition 5,000 esc per hour.

*Horse-riding*: 1,500 esc per hour.

*Tennis*: Quinta Magnolia 135 esc per hour; hotels 750-900 esc per hour.

**Swimming pools**. Lido: 190 esc (spectators 70 esc), sunshade hire 190 esc, lounger hire 190 esc; Quinta Magnolia: 130 esc; Barreirinha Lido: 125 esc; Savoy: 2,000 esc.

**Taxi**. 300 esc flat charge (includes first 1,200 metres) plus 70 esc per km out of town. Town to Hotel Zone approx 600 esc. At night (10pm and 7am) 300 esc flat charge which includes the first 500 metres.

**Toboggan Ride**. To Livramento 2,000 esc per person; to Funchal 4,000 esc per person.

## NEWSPAPERS and MAGAZINES *(jornal; revista)*

Europe's principal papers, including most British dailies, are on the news-stands the day after publication. Popular foreign magazines are sold at the same places. There is only one English language publication which includes any sort of what's on information, and that is the eccentrically-written, monthly, free newspaper, *The Madeira Island Bulletin* (also available in German, *Madeira Aktuell*). You can pick up a copy at the tourist office in Funchal. If you can understand a little Portuguese, the daily *Jornal da Madeira* newspaper gives you a weather forecast and museum and temporary exhibition details, among other things.

Have you any English-language newspapers/magazines? **Tem jornais/revistas em inglês?**

## OPENING HOURS

The Madeirans do not take a siesta, but most businesses close for a one- to two-hour lunch break. The list on the next page gives general times. See under the specific headings indicated for more detail:

**Banks**. 8:30am-3pm Monday-Friday (see also MONEY MATTERS on page 116); currency exchange offices 9am-1pm and 2-5pm Monday-Saturday (closed Saturday afternoon).

**Bars and restaurants**. Many bars are open from noon or earlier until the small hours. Café-restaurants may be open all day, whereas more up-market establishments will only open for the lunch and evening sessions. Some restaurants close one day a week to give staff a break.

**Funchal market**. 7am-4pm Monday-Thursday, 7am-8pm Friday, 7am-2pm Saturday.

**Museums**. Times and days vary, but most open at least between 10am and 5pm weekdays, several close 12:30-2pm. See *Jornal da Madeira* for up-to-date hours.

**Post offices**. Main Funchal office 9am-8pm Monday-Friday, local branches 9am-12:30pm and 2-6pm Monday-Friday (see also POST OFFICES on page 122).

**Shops**. Traditional shops 9am-1pm Monday-Saturday and 3-7pm Monday-Friday (closed Saturday afternoon). Shopping Centres 10am-11pm daily.

**Tourist Information Office**. Funchal office 9am-7pm Monday-Saturday, 9am-1pm Sunday. Other offices have shorter hours.

# P

## PHOTOGRAPHY

All popular brands, film types and accessories are sold in Funchal at competitive prices. Belafoto on Rua 31 de Janeiro is recommended. 24-hour processing is widely available for print films.

Field workers, fishermen and local people in general can make very photogenic subjects, but do ask before you snap. Most do not mind, but you may well offend elderly people. Remember that you are a guest in their country. Do not attempt to take photographs of military personnel or equipment (warships etc), or anywhere that it could be construed that you're breaching security.

| | |
|---|---|
| I'd like a film for this camera. | **Quero um rolo para esta máquina.** |
| May I take a picture? | **Posso tirar uma fotografia?** |

## POLICE *(polícia)*

The national police, wearing dark blue uniforms, maintain public order and oversee the traffic. The correct way to address any policeman is "Senhor Guarda."

| | |
|---|---|
| Where's the nearest police station? | **Onde fica o posto de polícia mais próximo?** |

**POST OFFICES** *(correios)* (See also TELEPHONES on page 125)

These are indicated by the letters CTT (*Correios, Telégrafos e Tele-fones*). You can buy stamps from shops as well as post offices. Most mail boxes follow the British pillar-box design. The opening hours of the main post office in Funchal are 8:30am-8pm Monday-Friday (9am-1pm Saturday). Local branches have shorter opening hours.

Telegrams *(telegrama)* can be sent from post offices, or you can give the text to your hotel receptionist. Most hotels have fax and telex facilities, as does the main post office.

| | |
|---|---|
| Where's the nearest post office? | **Onde fica a estação de correios mais próxima?** |
| express (special delivery) | **expresso** |
| registered | **registrado** |
| I want to send a telegram to ... | **Quero mandar um telegrama para ...** |

**Poste Restante** (*Posta Restante*). If you don't know where you'll be staying, you can have mail sent poste restante to any office convenient to you. For example: Mr. John Smith, Posta Restante, Funchal, Madeira, Portugal. You'll need to produce your passport when collecting mail.

**PUBLIC HOLIDAYS** *(feriado)*

The following list gives the national holidays of Portugal.

| January 1 | **Ano Novo** | New Year's Day |
|---|---|---|
| April 25 | **Dia da Liberdade** | Freedom Day |
| May 1 | **Dia do Trabalho** | Labour Day |
| June 10 | **Dia de Portugal** | National Day |
| August 15 | **Assunção** | Assumption |
| October 5 | **Dia da República** | Republic Day |
| November 1 | **Todos-os-Santos** | All Saints' Day |
| December 1 | **Restuaração/Dia da Independência** | Day of Restoration/ Independence |

| December 8 | **Imaculada Conceição** | Immaculate Conception |
| December 25 | **Natal** | Christmas Day |
| Movable dates: | **Carnaval** | Shrove Tuesday/Carnival |
| | **Sexta-feira Santa** | Good Friday |
| | **Corpo de Cristo** | Corpus Christi |

Madeira also celebrates 1 July (Discovery of the Island), 21 August (municipal holiday), and 26 December (Boxing Day).

| Are you open tomorrow? | **Estão abertos amanhã?** |

## PUBLIC TRANSPORT

**Buses** (*autocarro*). Most of the island can be covered by public buses, which are cheap, reliable, and generally run on time. The old bus station on Avenida do Mar has closed (though it is still marked on many maps). The five main bus companies have moved to new bus stations in different parts of the city. The tourist office has a leaflet on bus services and the routes and timetables are published in the English supplements to the *Noticias da Madeira* newspaper. Orange buses serve Funchal, while other coloured buses serve different parts of the island. As they sometimes bear the same number, things can get a little confusing. If you intend making several journeys, save money by buying a tourist pass valid for a week (or longer) available from bus stations. Otherwise buy your ticket on the bus. Bus stops are shown by the sign *paragem*.

There are no trains on Madeira; the last one departed permanently in 1939. The only other public transport you are likely to use is to get to Porto Santo. A catamaran crosses daily to Porto Santo (possibly slightly reduced timetable in winter), takes 90-105 minutes, and outside summer can be very bumpy (anti-sea sickness pills are recommended). The air shuttle takes just 15-20 minutes.

| Where is the nearest bus stop? | **Onde é a paragem de autocarros mais próxima?** |
| When's the next bus to ...? | **Quando parte o próximo autocarro para ...?** |

## Madeira

| I want a ticket to ... | **Queria um bilhete para ...** |
|---|---|
| single/return | **ida/ida e volta** |
| Will you tell me when | **Pode dizer-me quando** |
| to get off? | **devo descer?** |

# R

## RADIO and TV *(radio; televisão)*

Madeira has its own TV channel and also picks up Portuguese pro-
grammes. Most big hotels and some bars also have satellite TV for
screening football matches and other sporting events. For details of
what's on, pick up a copy of the *Jornal da Madeira* (see NEWSPAPERS
AND MAGAZINES on page 120). Tune into Tourist Radio (96 FM) for
news and features of tourist interest on the island, broadcast in several languages (English, 5:45-6:30pm Monday-Friday). The BBC
World Service and Voice of America can be heard on short-wave.

## RELIGION

The religion of Madeira is Roman Catholic. Anglican Sunday ser-
vices are conducted in Funchal's English Church on Rua da Quebra
Costas, and there is a Baptist Church on Rua Cidade de Honolulu.
The Scottish Kirk (Church), at the corner of Rua do Conselheiro and
Rua Ivens, has services on the first Sunday of each month. Times of
services are available from tourist offices and most hotels.

# T

## TAXIS *(táxi)*

Taxis are yellow and blue. Those within Funchal are metred, but for
journeys beyond the capital you will need to agree a fare with the driver
in advance. The savings can be quite substantial. Note that only taxis
with a "T" on the windscreen are approved by the tourist board and
covered by your own insurance. **If you are involved in an accident in
a taxi without a "T," your insurance may not cover you.** A list of

popular excursions and prices is kept at the tourist office, and each driver should also have one. For instance, the return fare from Funchal centre to Monte, taking in the Old Monte Gardens and the church, is 3,000 esc. Taxis can be hailed in the street. There is a fare supplement of 20% on weekends and holidays, and between 10pm and 7am.

| | |
|---|---|
| Where can I get a taxi? | **Onde posso encontrar um táxi?** |
| What's the fare to ... ? | **Quanto custa o percurso para ...?** |

## TELEPHONES *(telefone)*

Automatic coin and card telephones can be found in bars and restaurants and on the street. If you want to make international calls, buy a *Credifone* phonecard rather than fumbling with mountains of coins. The other alternative is to make your call from the post office, where you go to a booth and pay the person at the desk after the call. The cost of this is the same as a coin or card phone. You can, of course, phone from your hotel room, but this will cost at least double the normal price.

Dial 099 for the international operator for Europe, 098 for the rest of the world. For international direct dialling, use 00, followed by the area code (without the first 0) then the number. For directory enquiries within Madeira, dial 118.

**Telephone Spelling Code.** If the telephonist's English is poor and your own Portuguese basic, use the following town names instead of letters of the alphabet when spelling out words and names over the phone:

| | | | |
|---|---|---|---|
| A | Aveiro | N | Nazaré |
| B | Braga | O | Ovar |
| C | Coimbra | P | Porto |
| D | Dafundo | Q | Queluz |
| E | Évora | R | Rossio |
| F | Faro | S | Setúbal |
| G | Guarda | T | Tavira |
| H | Horta | U | Unidade |
| I | Itália | V | Vidago |

## Madeira

| | | | | |
|---|---|---|---|---|
| J | José | W | Wademar |
| K | Kodak | X | Xavier |
| L | Lisboa | Y | York |
| M | Maria | Z | Zulmira |

| | |
|---|---|
| Can you get me this number? | **Pode ligar-me para este número?** |
| reverse-charge (collect) call | **paga pelo destinatário** |
| person-to-person (personal) call | **com pré-aviso** |

## TIME DIFFERENCES

If travelling from Britain, do not adjust your watch as Madeira is on the same time.

**Summer time chart**.

| Los Angeles | Chicago | New York | London | Madeira |
|---|---|---|---|---|
| 4am | 6am | 7am | noon | **noon** |

## TIPPING

Hotel and restaurant bills are usually all-inclusive, so tipping is not obligatory. If the service has been good, however, you might like to give the following:

| | |
|---|---|
| Hairdresser | 10% |
| Hotel Maid, per week | 500-1,000 esc |
| Lavatory attendant | 25 esc |
| Hotel porter, per bag | 50-100 esc |
| Taxi driver | 10% |
| Waiter | 10% |
| Tour Guide | 10% or around 500 esc |

## TOILETS *(lavabos/toiletes)*

Public toilets in Funchal are few and far between, and never recommended. The best place to find a clean toilet is in a large hotel, but as there aren't any of these in the city centre, it's best to use a bar or restaurant (out of courtesy you should buy a drink, or at least ask permission). The "Ladies' is marked *Senhoras* and the "Gents" *Homens* or *Senhores*. Don't confuse *Senhoras* and *Senhores*!

## TOURIST INFORMATION OFFICES *(oficio do turismo)*

Information about Madeira is obtainable from Portuguese National Tourist Offices in many countries, including the following:

**Canada**: Suite 1005, 60 Bloor Street West, Toronto, Ontario M4W 3B8; tel. (416) 921-7376.

**United Kingdom**: 22/25a Sackville Street, London W1X 1DE; tel. (0171) 494 1441.

**USA**: 590 Fifth Avenue, 4th Floor, New York, NY 10036; tel. (212) 354 4403.

The tourist information offices in Funchal (22 90 57) and on Porto Santo (tel. 98 23 61) are staffed by assistants who are particularly helpful and speak English. If possible, always make the *turismo* your first stop, pick up the island/capital map, which locates all major points of interest.

The Funchal office stays open late from Monday to Saturday, while provincial offices keep more or less normal business hours. Aside from the Funchal office, there are two other Madeira branches, one at the airport and one in Machico. The future of a third branch, at Câmara de Lobos, is at present uncertain.

## TRAVELLERS WITH DISABILITIES

Both Madeira and Porto Santo airports are accessible to wheelchair users, but in general Madeira is very difficult for disabled travellers. Negotiating the busy, steep, cobbled streets of Funchal, for example, may pose problems, while, despite the recent boom in hotel building on the island, few places cater for wheelchair users. The only hotels that claim to be wheelchair friendly are the Savoy, Casino Park, Madeira Palácio, and Santa Isabel in Funchal (all 5-star except the last, which is 4-star), and the Hotel Atlantis in Machico (5-star). For more details, see *Holidays and Travel Abroad*, by RADAR, 12 City

## Madeira

Forum, 250 City Road, London EC1V 8AF; tel. 0171 250 3222. The
*A Rampa* restaurant in Funchal is also accessible.

Depending on your level of mobility, it should be feasible to tour
by taxi, but ordinary buses are inaccessible. Before you go, contact
the Holiday Care Service (tel. 01293 774535); they are experts in the
field of holidays for the disabled and will answer specific queries.

## WATER *(água)*

Madeiran water is safe to drink and doesn't taste bad either. Bottled
mineral water is sold cheaply everywhere; the Porto Santo brand has
a strong taste which is not to everyone's liking.

| | |
|---|---|
| a bottle of mineral water | **uma garrafa de água mineral** |
| sparkling (carbonated)/still | **com/sem gás** |

## WEIGHTS and MEASURES (For fluid and distance measures, see DRIVING on page 109)

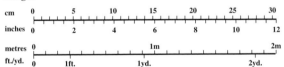

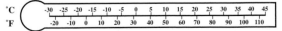

# Recommended Hotels

Below is a selection of hotels in different price bands, listed according to location, and then alphabetically. Book early for New Year, and for quintas, villas and pousadas throughout the year, as they have limited space (and also specify if you want to be in the old part). Telephone numbers and, where available, fax numbers, are given after each entry. The star rating in brackets after each hotel name refers to its official government grading (see page 104). As a guide to room prices, we have used the following symbols (for a double room with bath/shower in high season, including breakfast and VAT):

| | |
|---|---|
| ✪ | below 10,000 esc |
| ✪✪ | 10,000–15,000 esc |
| ✪✪✪ | 15,000–22,000 esc |
| ✪✪✪✪ | above 22,000 esc |

## FUNCHAL HOTEL ZONE

**Aparthotel Imperatriz (3-star)** ✪*Rua Imperatriz Dona Amélia, 72; Tel. 23 34 56; fax 22 95 58.* Reasonably-equipped studios with a rooftop pool, and a good restaurant. 27 self-catering apartments.

**Casino Park (5-star)** ✪✪✪✪ *Rua Imperatriz Dona Amélia; Tel. 23 31 11; fax 23 20 76.* A thoroughly modern, austere-looking complex in a magnificent location, set within its own gardens. The adjacent, popular casino is the focus for a lively entertainment programme. 327 rooms.

**Cliff Bay Hotel (5-star)** ✪✪✪✪ *Estrada Monumental, 147; Tel. 07 07 07; fax 76 25 25.* Magnificent new hotel with sea views from nearly all its 201 rooms. Excellent facilities including 2 pools and a tennis court.

**Madeira Carlton (5-star)** ✪✪✪✪ *Largo António Nobre; Tel. 23 10 31; fax 22 33 77.* An attractive complex spanning a river gorge adjacent to the famous Reid's Hotel, with direct views of the ocean. It offers several restaurants and lively night-life. A tennis court, two swimming pools, other sports facilities. 375 rooms.

**Madeira Regency Club (4-star)** ✪✪✪*Rua Carvalho Araújo; Tel. 23 23 44; fax 23 23 74.* These spacious and well-equipped poolside apartments come with sun terraces and access to the sea. The staff are exceptionally friendly. Facilities include a sauna and squash courts. 92 rooms (part of a larger time-share complex).

**Quinta da Penha de França (4-star Albergaria)** ✪✪ *Rua da Penha de França; Tel. 22 90 80; fax 22 92 61.* This *albergaria* occupies what is possibly Funchal's most beautiful *quinta* setting, hidden in a lovely garden with a terrace, piano bar, outdoor dining, lawn and its own swimming pool. A new extension is currently being built down to sea level. 41 rooms.

**Quinta do Sol (4-star)** ✪✪✪ *Rua Dr. Pita, 6; Tel. 76 41 51; fax 76 62 87.* A highly rated and well-equipped modern hotel (not a *quinta*) next to the lovely Quinta Magnolia Park, but also on a busy traffic junction. Swimming pool. 151 rooms.

**Quinta Perestrello (4-star Estalagem)** ✪✪-✪✪✪ *Rua Dr. Pita, 3; Tel. 76 23 33; fax 76 37 77.* Charming, 150-year old country house. Lovely garden and swimming pool. Close to Quinta Magnolia, but adjacent to a busy road junction. 28 rooms.

**Reid's (5-star)** ✪✪✪✪ *Estrada Monumental, 139; Tel. 76 30 01; fax 76 44 99.* The quintessential hotel for the English abroad, sumptuously redecorated in July 1993; luxurious and boasting magnificent gardens. Spacious sun terraces, swimming pools, tennis courts. 173 rooms.

**Savoy (5-star)** ✪✪✪✪ *Avenida do Infante; Tel. 22 20 31; fax 22 31 03.* The Savoy Hotel's unprepossessing exterior belies the opulence of its public rooms. Luxuriant gardens lead down to a well-equipped lido. Two tennis courts, nightclub. 350 rooms.

**Vila Camacho (3-star Residencial)** ✪ *Beco da Amoreira, 26, Avenida Estados Unidos da América; Tel. 76 54 59.* Two traditional houses providing simple but informal and pleasant accommodation set in a quiet location on a hill above the hustle and bustle of the town. Run by friendly owners. 25 rooms.

## FUNCHAL TOURIST ZONE

**Aparthotel Carlton Palms (4-star)** ✪✪✪ *Rua do Gorgulho, 15; Tel. 76 61 00; fax 76 62 47.* A brand new hotel right on the seafront, which at the same time incorporates a refurbished *quinta* within. All rooms are elegantly furnished, self-catering studios. Swimming pool, health club, gymnasium. 90 studios.

**Aparthotel Eden Mar (4-star)** ✪✪✪ *Rua do Gorgulho, 2; Tel. 76 22 21; fax 76 19 66.* A well-equipped, popular, modern aparthotel set in a busy location in the heart of the Tourist Zone. Pleasant garden. Facilities include swimming pool, gym, squash, sauna. 140 apartments.

**Aparthotel Gorgulho (3-star)** ✪✪ *Rua do Gorgulho, 1; Tel. 76 10 11; fax 76 32 83.* This rather ugly high-rise block hides an attractive secluded terrace and swimming pools. Rooms are simply furnished and some are equipped with self-catering facilities. Facilities include sauna, solarium, tennis court. 115 rooms.

**Girassol (4-star)** ✪✪ *Estrada Monumental, 256; Tel. 76 40 51; fax 76 54 41.* Modern hotel, pleasant, popular, and friendly, located on the busy main Funchal highway, but with a secluded garden and swimming pool. 133 rooms.

**Vila Vicencia (4-star Residencial)** ✪ *Caminho Velho da Ajuda, 45; Tel. 76 15 27.* A charming family-run establishment comprising three adjacent houses, Vila Vicencia is situated only a 5-minute walk away from the Lido complex. It has a lovely small garden with a private swimming pool. 28 rooms.

# FUNCHAL TOWN

### Apartamentos Turísticos do Castanheiro (2-star) ✪
*Rua do Castanheiro, 21–29; Tel. 22 70 60; fax 22 79 40.*
Brand new apartments in an excellent location Just off Praça
do Município. Well-equipped rooms, friendly staff and very
good value. Recommended snack-bar restaurant adjacent. 24
apartments.

## OTHER LOCATIONS

### Atlantic Gardens (4-star) ✪✪ *Praia Formosa; Tel. 76 21 11;*
*fax 76 67 33.* A short distance (3 km/2 miles) from the Lido, this
new aparthotel enjoys an exclusive beach-side location and
views to Cabo Girão. Well-equipped rooms, swimming pool. 53
apartments.

### Casa do Caseiro (4-star Residencial) ✪ *Caminho do*
*Monte, 62; Tel. 22 90 31.* Set high above Funchal, halfway down
the Monte toboggan run, this charming small house has been
sympathetically restored and comes with use of its small swimming pool. Eight rooms.

### Pousada dos Vinháticos (3-star Pousada) ✪-✪✪ *Serra*
*de Água, (23 miles/37 km from Funchal); Tel. 95 23 44; fax 95*
*25 40.* Government-owned hotel enjoying a splendid (roadside)
location with mountain views. Simple but comfortable rooms.
12 rooms.

### Quinta da Bela Vista (5-star Estalagem) ✪✪-✪✪✪
*Caminho do Avista Navios, 4; Tel. 76 41 44; fax 76 50 90.* 150-
year old family-run hotel 3 km (2 miles) west of town with
splendid views. Beautiful rooms, excellent food. Small gym and
sauna, swimming pool. 68 rooms.

### Vila Ramos (4-star) ✪✪✪ *Azinhaga da Casa Branca, 7; Tel.*
*76 41 81; fax 76 41 56.* Modern hotel in a quiet location, 15-
minutes' walk (3 km/2 miles) from the Lido (daily mini-bus to
town). Tennis, gym, sauna, swimming pool. 116 rooms.

# Recommended Restaurants

We appreciated the food and service in the restaurants listed below. If you find other places that you think are worth recommending, we'd be pleased to hear from you. Entries are listed according to location, and then alphabetically. To give you an idea of price (for a three-course meal per person, excluding drinks and service) we have used the following symbols:

| | |
|---|---|
| ✪ | under 2,200 esc |
| ✪✪ | 2,200–3,500 esc |
| ✪✪✪ | over 3,500 esc |

## FUNCHAL TOWN

**Carochina** ✪ *Rua Sao Francisco, 2A; Tel. 22 36 95.* Situated around the corner from the Tourist Office, offering excellent value.

**O Celeiro** ✪✪✪ *Rua dos Aranhas, 22; Tel. 23 06 22.* Highly-rated, rustic cellar restaurant. Seafood and *cataplana* are among the house specialities.

**Dos Combatentes** ✪ *Rua Ivens, 1; Tel. 22 13 88.* A modest local place to eat, near the São Francisco gardens. Serves typical Madeiran and Portuguese dishes.

**Golfinho** ✪✪✪ *Largo do Corpo Santo, 21; Tel. 22 67 74.* One of the best known and most popular of the Old Town restaurants, where smoked swordfish and *caldeirada* are two of the favourites. Free bus service.

**Jacquet** ✪ *Rua de Santa Maria, 5; No telephone reservations.* A locals' "hole-in-the-wall" establishment, where an open kitchen serves eight formica-topped tables at a time. Sample the *caramujos* (winkles) and *cavala* (mackerel).

**O Pitéu** ✪ *Rua da Carreira, 182A; Tel. 22 08 19.* Serving an excellent range of *cozinha típica caseira*, and featuring Portuguese and Madeiran dishes seldom seen on restaurant menus. *Fado* and guitar music on both Tuesday (9pm-midnight) and Friday (10pm-2am). Closed Monday evening and Sunday.

**Tavira** ✪ *Rua da Queimada da Cima, 27; Tel. 22 35 07.* Small relaxed restaurant popular with locals and tourists. Standard Madeiran menu with variations.

## FUNCHAL HOTEL ZONE

**Casa dos Reis** ✪✪✪ *Rua da Penha de França, 6; Tel. 22 51 82.* Attractive small, formal restaurant, serving a wide range of international, French and Portuguese dishes. Try the fish terrine in saffron jelly, rolled espada with green pepper sauce and flambé special. Dinner only.

**Casa Velha** ✪✪✪ *Rua Imperatriz Dona Amélia, 69; Tel. 22 57 49.* A formal restaurant in an intimate, 19th-century setting with revolving ceiling fans and *azulejo* decor. The small international-Madeiran menu attracts a strong following. Try *espada flambé* with champagne. Piano music.

**Joe's Bar** ✪ *Quinta da Penha de França, Rua da Penha de França; Tel. 22 90 87.* Eat on the lovely garden terraces or in an attractive dining room. Limited menu, but look out for the dish of the day.

**Kon Tiki** ✪✪ *Rua do Favila, 9; Tel. 76 47 37.* Offering an interesting menu of Madeiran favourites with an international twist, as well as specialities from Finland (fillet steak on hot stone). Closed Monday.

**Quinta Magnolia** ✪ *Quinta Magnolia, Rua Dr. Pita, 10; Tel. 76 40 13 (booking essential, accepted up to 2 days in advance).* This quinta in the park is home to the Madeira Hotel School, which serves up four-course Portuguese lunches in the dining room previously used by the British Country Club. Excellent value. Lunchtime only, closed Sunday.

**A Rampa** ✪✪ *Avenida Infante Ed. Henrique II; Tel. 23 52 75.* Smart, popular restaurant with a pleasant conservatory and outdoor terrace. Extensive international-Madeiran menu, plus pizza and pasta. Try either *arroz de mariscos* or *fritura mista*. Good service. Wheelchair access.

## FUNCHAL TOURIST ZONE

**Gavina's** ✪✪✪ *Rua do Gorgulho (Praia); Tel. 76 29 18.* A local legend for its fish dishes, served in a simply furnished dining room which overlooks the sea. Free bus service.

**Lido Mar** ✪ *Lido Complex; Tel. 76 43 69.* Tasty, good value lunch. Choose your meat to barbecue, and by the time you have heaped your plate with salad, it'll be cooked.

**O Porco em Pé** ✪✪ *Estrada Monumental, 356; Tel. 76 21 11.* As the name ("The Pig's Trotter") suggests, pork is the speciality of this rustic-style restaurant.

**Tropical** ✪✪✪ *Hotel Florasol, Estrada Monumental, 306; Tel. 76 36 42.* One of Funchal's favourite restaurants, with a popular international-Madeiran menu which is famous for its *flambé* desserts. Live music every night. Free bus service.

## OUTSIDE FUNCHAL

**Montanha Grill** ✪✪ *Estrada Nacional, 101, São Gonçalo; Tel. 79 35 00.* Big rustic-style *churrasco* restaurant, serving wholesome portions of meat. Fine views over Funchal.

**A Praia** ✪-✪✪ *Praia, Câmara de Lobos; Tel. 94 23 54.* Simple beach restaurant, long appreciated by the locals for its excellent value. Try the *tamboril* (angler fish/monkfish).

**Santo António** ✪ *Estreito-Câmara de Lobos; Tel. 94 54 39.* A well-known, friendly, bustling restaurant, serving *cozinha típica caseira*. Espetada is the most popular pick of a short menu.

**Victor's Bar (The Old Trout Inn)** ✪✪ *Ribeira Frio; Tel. 78 28 98.* A cosy bar reminiscent of an English pub leads to a chalet-like dining area with open fires. Trout is the house speciality.

# ABOUT BERLITZ

In 1878 Professor Maximilian Berlitz had a revolutionary idea about making language learning accessible and enJoyable. One hundred and twenty years later these same principles are still successfully at work.

For language instruction, translation and interpretation services, cross-cultural training, study abroad programs, and an array of publishing products and additional services, visit any one of our more than 350 Berlitz Centers in over 40 countries.

Please consult your local telephone directory for the Berlitz Center nearest you or visit our web site at http://www.berlitz.com.

**Helping the World Communicate**